A HUMAN

It seemed an almost impossible task. There was no way to tell if the gruesome jumbled-up contents of the garbage bags were one victim or several victims without piecing them back together.

Dr. Mary Anne Clayton and her staff at the Bergen County, N.J., medical examiner's office were up to the job. They logged the 68 body parts the police had found in the trunks of two cars. They laid out the head, limbs, and organs, all of which appeared to have been removed with surgical precision. There were enough pieces for just one victim, a male. The man's skull, although split, was still in one piece. Sheriff's divers had recovered the lips and nose. They were placed on the facial area and photographed to aid in identification.

Stiff, jagged fingertip shavings had been in one of the bags and they were now carefully matched to the fingers of the body's severed hands. Although someone had taken a great deal of care to remove the fingerprints, the man's jaw had been left with its teeth intact. An impression was made so that they could be compared with the dental records of the missing research scientist.

His name was Yakov Gluzman—a brilliant molecular biologist who thought he had escaped the brutality of Russia to find the American Dream.

He was wrong.

<u>BOOK YOUR PLACE ON OUR WEBSITE</u> AND MAKE THE <u>READING CONNECTION!</u>

We've created a customized website just for our very special readers, where you can get the inside scoop on everything that's going on with Zebra, Pinnacle and Kensington books.

When you come online, you'll have the exciting opportunity to:

- View covers of upcoming books

- Read sample chapters

- Learn about our future publishing schedule (listed by publication month *and author*)

- Find out when your favorite authors will be visiting a city near you

- Search for and order backlist books from our online catalog

- Check out author bios and background information

- Send e-mail to your favorite authors

- Meet the Kensington staff online

- Join us in weekly chats with authors, readers and other guests

- Get writing guidelines

- AND MUCH MORE!

Visit our website at
http://www.pinnaclebooks.com

SEVERED RELATIONS

Tim Hays

Pinnacle Books
Kensington Publishing Corp.
http://www.pinnaclebooks.com

Some names have been changed to protect the privacy of individuals connected to this story.

PINNACLE BOOKS are published by

Kensington Publishing Corp.
850 Third Avenue
New York, NY 10022

Pinnacle and the P logo Reg. U.S. Pat. & TM Off.

First Printing: July, 1998
10 9 8 7 6 5 4 3

Printed in the United States of America

One

Early Easter Sunday morning in April, 1996, just before 10:30 A.M., Officer Richard Freeman of the East Rutherford Police Department was on routine patrol in the sleepy New Jersey town eight miles west of New York City. A working class suburb, East Rutherford is a former factory town with clusters of aging homes, some service stations, a Dunkin' Donuts, and a rundown bowling alley. While some of its residents were on their way to eleven o'clock mass across town, Freeman decided to drive through a small industrial park at the end of Madison Street on the city's south side, a nondescript series of two-floor office buildings fronting the Passaic River three miles west of the Meadowlands sports complex. Freeman made frequent patrols down Madison and throughout the five-square-mile town. As this was a holiday Sunday, he did not expect many workers or visitors to be within the three-acre industrial park at One Madison.

Around 10:40 A.M. Freeman, a fourteen-year veteran of the town's police force and one of two East Rutherford officers on patrol this particularly gray, raw morning, came upon a blue Ford Taurus parked in the rear of the industrial park's lot. It was noticeable for being the only car in the section of the One lot nearest the bank of the Passaic River. Normally, on a workday, forty or so cars and trucks would be parked within. The Taurus was parked backward toward the Passaic, its rear facing the edge of the parking lot's six-foot drop to the water. Its trunk was open, which Freeman thought strange. He pulled his cruiser next to the car, and started to run its plates when a man came running up from the riverbank toward the Taurus. The man had a frightened look on his face, and it looked to Freeman as though he had just thrown some debris into the water.

This wasn't just some fisherman, Freeman thought, like the guys he'd see holding lines from the rear of the Madison complex parking lot on weekends. The cop's eye caught some rather prominent bloodstains on the man's hands, and sensed something unusual about the man now racing frantically up the hill toward him.

Cautiously, Freeman confronted the man, who suddenly started to reach into the pocket of his brown leather jacket. Freeman had already positioned his own right hand on his holstered service revolver, then quickly reached and grabbed the startled man's hand inside his jacket pocket, squeezing it until he submitted. The officer was relieved not to feel a weapon underneath. Ordering the man to stand still, Freeman asked for his license and registration, and learned he was thirty-nine-year-old Vladimir Zelenin.

While Zelenin stood against the Taurus, the officer ran the man's license and car registration, discovering that the ten-year-old sedan was registered to ECI Technologies, one of the small offices in the One Madison complex. There were no arrest warrants for Zelenin. As Freeman scanned the front of the Taurus, he noticed several household garbage bags with something inside them laying on the passenger seat and, probable cause having been established, he curiously began looking through them as he kept one eye on Zelenin. The officer found a Playtex glove, a shower curtain, and a scrub brush in one bag; a hacksaw, an ax, a hatchet, and a set of expensive kitchen knives in the other. Zelenin offered little resistance to Freeman's search. He had been overwhelmed by the six-foot-two, 225-pound policeman's interruption of his dumping and was aware of the authority of uniformed officials. Freeman handcuffed Zelenin, read him his Miranda rights, then seated the man in the back of his cruiser and radioed for the other East Rutherford officer on patrol that morning, Todd McQuade.

When McQuade arrived three minutes later, Freeman resumed searching the Taurus, looking into the trunk of the car while McQuade kept an eye on the handcuffed Zelenin. Freeman made a startling discovery: the debris he deduced Zelenin had been throwing into the Passaic—small parcels in other household trash bags in the Taurus's trunk—was bloody, as the man's hands had been. It was becoming clear to the officer why Zelenin had become so nervous when Freeman surprised him. Freeman opened one of the green bags and discovered flesh, then what appeared to him to be a gall bladder and a liver. Although a polluted body of water for years, the environmental and litter laws in New Jersey prohibit disposing of any garbage in the Garden State's waterways, even the wretched Passaic.

"Todd, this isn't animal guts," Freeman said to McQuade.

When Freeman looked into another bag and found a human skull, skinned of its face and recently dead, as the other body parts were, the officer knew this was going to be a long day.

Freeman and McQuade called East Rutherford police headquarters on Uhland Street a mile away, and informed the desk officer, Jerome Winston, of their discovery and of the potentially serious crime at hand. Winston notified the other officers working the holiday shift at the station house, then beeped both the chief of the detective division, Captain Ken Felton, and the head of the twenty-three-member department, Chief John LaGraca, and found the department's two highest-ranking officials on their way to mass. As Felton and LaGraca raced to One Madison, Winston began to call the other support personnel in Bergen County who normally respond to matters involving a potential capital crime.

Freeman questioned Zelenin as he awaited the arrival of the backup officials. The nervous man quickly began to "turn," as Freeman would later say, almost anxious to say something to the officer, who now considered the man a suspect in some crime. Zelenin wasn't offering any protest of his innocence. Although he'd nodded in the affirmative when read his Miranda rights in English, it became obvious to Freeman that Zelenin spoke limited English, and was apparently Slavic. Freeman radioed for a Polish translator, knowing there were many emigrated Poles in the northeast New Jersey towns nearby, and thinking Zelenin possibly to be one of them. The prisoner looked up from his seat at the officer and exclaimed, in frail, broken English, "No, *Russian*. I speak Russian!" Freeman immediately radioed back to Uhland Street, and asked Winston to call the FBI and request a translator from the Bureau's Newark office who could rush to the site.

Waiting for the others, Freeman asked his prisoner, "Vladimir, are these parts from a human body?"

"Yes," Zelenin replied.

"Well, are they male or female, Vladimir?"

"Male."

"Whose are they?" Freeman started to ask, before his prisoner interrupted him.

"More, more," the man said, as he wiggled his hands, which were cuffed behind his back. Motioning to Freeman, he pointed toward the far end of the parking lot.

"More what?" Freeman asked.

"More parts."

Freeman looked down the lot to a Nissan Maxima sixty feet away, parked between a trash dumpster and a yellow Ryder rental truck, and asked the prisoner if he meant the car.

"Yes," Zelenin said. While Freeman and McQuade watched him carefully, the man struggled with his cuffed hands for the Nissan's keys in the front pocket of his worn leather jacket.

What Freeman discovered in the Maxima's trunk was as grotesque as what he'd seen in the Taurus. As he waited for the other crime scene personnel, who were starting to arrive, the officer recovered three more trash bags from the second car, all filled with body parts. Chief LaGraca and the detective commander, Felton, were first, and once the chief ordered Madison Street closed at the entrance to the office park to protect what was an enormous crime scene, the other arriving uniformed officers erected barricades to prevent the growing number of curious citizens on lower Madison Street from interrupting their work. A television news van was turned back at the cordon. Minutes later LaGraca and Felton were joined by Dr. Mary Anne Clayton, the youthful deputy medical examiner of Bergen County, and her assistant, Coleen McVeigh, who had been rushed from their offices in Paramus by county police. Then came a van carrying three scuba divers from the Bergen County Sheriff's Office, summoned just before noon at their Hackensack station to retrieve possible evidence from the Passaic River. After a briefing, the first of the divers braved the murky, littered, thirty-five-degree water searching for anything resembling a human body part, returning from the clouded water five minutes later with a large hand, which Clayton noticed was missing its fingerprints. The next diver handed McVeigh a nose attached to a set of lips. Finally, Clayton and her assistant identified a right forearm and a left foot, both apparently male, and a left upper arm, from the last diver out of the water near the Taurus.

Officer Freeman was beginning to feel ill at the sight of the body parts. Fortunately, he thought, the carp and catfish in the river fortified by years of industrial pollution hadn't yet eaten the evidence, which Clayton and McVeigh were carefully wrapping and assembling in the bright yellow disaster pouches the two coroners carried in their official bags for identification and autopsy of bodies. By the time Sergeant Tom Goldrick, the senior homicide investigator from the Bergen County District Attorney's Office who'd had the rotation that morning, arrived, the crime scene, though busy with forty or so public safety officials milling about, was under control.

Whenever a major crime is committed in East Rutherford or any of the thirty towns and cities within Bergen County, the local police call the district attorney's office. When Goldrick was summoned with a loud beep while at mass with his family twenty minutes north, he quickly left alone and drove to the scene. Bergen County Investigators, or BCI, as his elite detective squad was known, didn't beep its eight homicide investigators on a whim. Less than two hours after Freeman's diligent patrol had accidentally discovered and arrested Zelenin, a full contingent of Bergen County law enforcement personnel was present in the industrial park. Now it would be left to Goldrick to assemble the reports from the local officers and detectives, the sheriff's divers, and finally the man in custody as the investigator began to ascertain the magnitude of the crime.

By two o'clock, the uniformed officers started to load the two cars onto a sheriff's department flatbed truck for the short drive to the East Rutherford garage. Mary Anne Clayton and Coleen McVeigh tagged the five body parts they had collected from the divers, who had completed their sweep of the near-freezing Passaic, and were looking inside the trash bags at the other pieces. Like the detectives who were waiting to dust the cars for fingerprints, the coroner could only wrap the garbage bags in protective covering until the ERPD detectives were granted a search warrant from a judge in Hackensack, the county seat, before cataloging any more parts of the gruesome puzzle they had begun to assemble. McQuade and Goldrick took the handcuffed Zelenin to the East Rutherford station house with Captain Felton,

while Officer Freeman stayed behind with Captain John
Taschler, an East Rutherford commander, to maintain
the parking lot crime scene.

The news radio reports on AM stations WCBS and
WINS early Sunday afternoon informed the tri-state
metropolitan area surrounding New York City that a
man had been arrested throwing parts of a body into
the Passaic River near the Meadowlands. Another report
erroneously claimed the police discovered a Russian
man with parts from eleven bodies. Across the river,
facing the rear of the office park, on New Jersey Route
21, a number of TV vans were positioned on the outer
shoulder of the highway, their crews desperately trying
to see what the police were doing 150 yards away while
searching for a clip that might lead their evening tele-
casts, normally quiet on Easter.

Freeman made time for one personal phone call.
"I'm running real late," he told his brother, who had
invited the recently divorced Freeman for Easter supper
with his family in northern New Jersey. "So have dinner
without me. I got a case with body parts, and I might
not be too hungry later on anyway."

Inside the East Rutherford police headquarters, the
officers who had remained at the station house stretched
their necks so they could see the suspect being led
in by Officer McQuade and Sergeant Goldrick. ERPD
didn't see many potential murder suspects in a given
year. All were aware now of the severity of the case, and
they knew that sooner or later Goldrick, with his cool
demeanor and the professional confidence that came
from years of working on serious cases, would elicit

from the mysterious, disheveled suspect the full story surrounding the mysterious body parts he'd tried to dump in the river. Vladimir Zelenin had twice acknowledged his Miranda rights, but wished to make a statement.

As they sat in the ERPD detective squad room, it seemed to Goldrick, as it had four hours before to Freeman, that their prisoner wanted desperately to get something off his chest, even to the extent of waiving legal counsel before talking to the detective. It was 3 P.M. when Goldrick began his interview of Zelenin. They had waited for the FBI's Russian interpreter, Agent Gary Dixon, to arrive. Dixon had been chased down by the agent-in-charge of the Bureau's Newark office on his day off. Now, as the three men sat in the East Rutherford holding room, Goldrick felt he might begin to make progress in identifying the victim.

"Whose body is it we found in the car, Mr. Zelenin?" Goldrick asked.

Zelenin's direct answer in English came across with a broken syntax to Goldrick.

"Body is Yakov Gluzman. He is scientist. We killed him in Pearl River."

"We?" asked Goldrick.

"We, me and Rita, his wife."

Goldrick carefully took notes. "Rita? The deceased's wife is named Rita Gluzman?"

"Yes." Then the prisoner proceeded to tell Goldrick and Dixon a grisly story.

Rita Gluzman had forced him to kill her husband Yakov, he said. She threatened to have him deported to Kyrgyzstan, his native country in the former Soviet Union, near the confluence of the republic's borders with China and Pakistan, where he would surely be killed, as the anti-Semitism there was frightening to Jews,

Zelenin told them, and he was Jewish. The anti-Semites had killed his wife three years earlier, he said, and he'd taken their two sons to the United States for safety. He'd landed in Brooklyn and stayed with his cousin, a man named Gregory Kogan, when not long after he'd met Rita Gluzman, a Ukrainian who was their mutual cousin, and her husband Yakov. He'd eventually been able to find a job working for Rita at ECI Technologies, the company she controlled in the business park at One Madison. Rita had threatened to have him deported if he didn't kill Yakov.

"Why would she want to kill Yakov?" Goldrick asked.

"To stop the divorce. Yakov left Rita, and she didn't want that," said the shivering Zelenin.

Was he here legally? Was he in any way connected to the growing "Russian mafia" that had begun to make its presence felt in the New York area? Had this been a mob hit by anyone?

Zelenin said he had been granted political asylum in the United States by the Immigration and Naturalization Service, and that he was not part of any organized crime syndicate. He'd killed the victim only because he'd been forced to, by the victim's wife, Rita. It wasn't business, it was personal. He'd been backed into a corner, he told them. Then she'd run out on him, leaving him to be arrested, after he had risked his life to help her.

Goldrick nodded, continuing his questioning through Dixon. The Bergen investigator thought to himself, this guy killed a man, chopped him into little pieces, because the man's wife told him to? All because she couldn't get a good divorce lawyer? Curious, he thought, particularly in a no-fault state like New Jersey.

Vladimir Zelenin was getting more comfortable talking with the affable Goldrick. The man continued his story.

He and Rita had gone to Yakov Gluzman's apartment, about twenty miles away in Pearl River, New York, just over the border north of New Jersey, the night before. They had huddled inside the apartment with the weapons for nearly seven hours, waiting for Dr. Gluzman to get home from his job as a scientist at a nearby pharmaceutical laboratory. When Yakov entered his apartment at around 11:30 Saturday night, just before the clocks changed, Zelenin said he and Rita had struck her husband in the head with the ax and the hatchet that were on the front seat of the Taurus in the bags with the body parts. Yakov was killed almost instantly. Using the Henckel kitchen knives and hacksaw, Rita and he had spent the night cutting up the body in the bathtub of the apartment, and in the morning they'd packed Yakov's dissected body into the garbage bags they'd brought with them, then hauled the bags out to Zelenin's Taurus and the Maxima, which belonged to Yakov, parked in the rear lot of his apartment complex. Zelenin said he and Rita Gluzman had then driven to East Rutherford, where they intended to dump the body in the river in back of her office. When the two killers arrived at One Madison, Rita had Zelenin drive her to her home in Upper Saddle River in order to have an alibi, Zelenin continued, as Yakov was supposed to visit her Sunday morning. He then returned to One Madison to dispose of the bloody bags.

Goldrick had noticed several bandages on Zelenin's right hand that seemed to cover a wound between the man's thumb and index finger.

"How did that happen?" the detective asked.

He had gotten cut by Rita's ax as they struck Yakov, Zelenin told him. On the way back to New Jersey, they had stopped at a CVS drugstore to buy some bandages, and Rita had wrapped his wound.

Goldrick had thought he'd seen and heard a lot during his thirteen years on the force. But this was a truly gruesome story. The detective had worked on more than fifteen murder cases, and had assisted on a few more working homicide at the Bergen DA's office. Now, he thought, why hadn't Zelenin just shot Yakov, if this collection of body parts being catalogued over at the coroner's office was truly his? Why had he hacked him up into so many pieces? There were certainly plenty of cleaner ways to kill someone. And why dump the body near the killer's workplace? Why not in the woods somewhere?

Zelenin started to tell Goldrick. "I couldn't find a gun," he said. "And I knew the body parts would sink into the river."

Goldrick was still perplexed.

"Yakov was too big to carry out in one piece," Zelenin said.

As he looked out the second floor window of the East Rutherford detective division while contemplating Sergeant Goldrick's questions, Zelenin saw the Maxima atop the flatbed truck slowly being wheeled with his Taurus into the station house parking lot. Zelenin turned to Goldrick, excitedly, and said, in broken English, ignoring Dixon, "Fingerprints on cars. Rita's prints. Get off cars. Don't tell Rita I'm tell you this."

Nobody at East Rutherford had been able to reach Rita Gluzman, whom Zelenin had told the cops was the wife of the victim, and who he'd further claimed had been with him when he'd killed the victim. The cops had found a listing for Gluzman in Upper Saddle River, a wealthy suburb of Bergen County about ten miles northwest. But the police had not found anyone at the number listed. They'd tried the number listed for a

Yakov Gluzman in Pearl River, New York, and had gotten only an answering machine.

Zelenin had no idea where Rita had gone, if she wasn't at home.

By 6 P.M., Goldrick's attempts to locate either Yakov or Rita Gluzman were still fruitless. Goldrick called his Bergen Homicide colleague, senior investigator Carlos Rodriguez, and brought him up to date on the interrogation of Vladimir Zelenin. Rodriguez drove to the Gluzman home, ten minutes from his Hackensack office, to see if either of the Gluzmans were home, and alive.

When Rodriguez arrived at the Gluzman home late Sunday evening, the detective found a contingent of police officers from the Upper Saddle River department waiting outside the Gluzman home, which was in a mile-square development of well-kept homes on one-acre parcels. Rodriguez and the township police inquired and found Ilan Gluzman, twenty-five, the Gluzmans' son, who told them he hadn't seen his mother since early that morning, and he didn't know where she was or when Rita planned to return.

"What is the problem?" Ilan nervously asked the detective. Then he told Rodriguez, "My father hasn't lived here since last fall." His parents had separated, Ilan said, and Yakov Gluzman had taken a small apartment in Pearl River, New York, just north and east of Upper Saddle River, close to his place of work, Lederle Laboratories. Ilan volunteered to go to Pearl River with Rodriguez and see if his father was okay, and the two men set off on the twenty-minute drive while the other policemen stayed behind at the Gluzman home, in the event either Rita or Yakov appeared. When Ilan and Rodriguez arrived at the Celia Gardens apartment complex on Middletown Road, the two men walked upstairs to Yakov's apartment when the detective almost immediately noticed a blood trail on the carpet outside the doorway. They appeared to be very fresh stains positioned in a line that suggested to Rodriguez a path out of the apartment into the hallway and downstairs, as opposed to one leading into it. Joined by officers from the Orangetown, New York Police Department who'd been briefed about the situation, the contingent entered Yakov Gluzman's apartment but found it empty and, moreover, clean. It wasn't evident that a crime had occurred inside, but the Rockland Sheriff's Department sealed the apartment with crime scene tape as Rodriguez mulled over the bloodstains outside. Ilan Gluzman was shaking, and asked the Bergen detective again what was happening.

Rodriguez waited until he confirmed his suspicions about the blood leading from Yakov Gluzman's apartment and had spoken with Goldrick, who was still questioning Vladimir Zelenin, before confronting the Gluzmans' son with the disturbing news that his father might have been the victim of foul play, once they had returned to the Gluzman home in New Jersey. Ilan shook and was obviously devastated at learning his father might have been murdered. The young man wondered aloud where his mother had been all day.

Back in East Rutherford, Tom Goldrick had determined after several hours of interviewing his prisoner that the murder of the person whose dismembered body was in the New Jersey police garage waiting to be organized by the coroner most likely had been committed in Rockland County, in New York State. During a break in his questioning of Zelenin early Sunday evening, Goldrick called the Orangetown PD and the Rockland County District Attorney's Office, where the night duty officer there paged investigator Jim Stewart and First Assistant District Attorney Lou Valvo. Stewart, commanding officer of the Rockland DA's major-case detectives, was at home. He assigned a senior detective, Steve Colantonio, to join him for the drive to East Rutherford to look into a possible homicide that had been committed in Rockland. Valvo, meanwhile, had been beeped while driving home on the Cross-Bronx Expressway from Easter dinner at his parents' home on Long Island. The DA drove his wife and infant son home, then raced off to the Uhland Street station house to join Stewart, Colantonio, and Detective Tom Hoffmann of Orangetown PD in the questioning of Vladimir Zelenin. Goldrick had assembled the group to determine where jurisdiction lay, in New Jersey or New York.

Goldrick knew this was a big case. He was trying to figure out, though, just why Zelenin was so talkative, so cooperative with the police. The suspect had waived his Miranda rights in two languages. Why was this man spilling his guts so easily? Goldrick asked himself.

The crowd at East Rutherford looking in on Zelenin's questioning late Sunday night was now resembling something like the gallery at the eighteenth hole of the U.S. Open. Captain Felton talked with Valvo, Hoffmann, Stewart, and Colantonio, the Rockland contingent, while Goldrick wrapped up his eight-hour interrogation of Zelenin, who told the men he hadn't slept in almost two days. Weary from the questioning, Zelenin refused to be videotaped repeating his confession.

One of the two jurisdictions present would have to formally take the case. Taking into account where the crime originated and where the victim's body was found, the East Rutherford chiefs conferred just before twelve and told Goldrick and Valvo: Rockland would get the case. Zelenin would be booked at the Bergen County jail while the New York authorities sought extradition of the prisoner, who was now an admitted participant in a capital crime.

As Sunday turned into Monday, and with their questioning of Zelenin now completed, Goldrick and Valvo put out a radio call for a nationwide alert throughout the New York region, which would be heard by police departments, sheriffs' offices, the FBI, and transportation authorities at airports, and train and bus stations: Rita Gluzman, forty-eight, was wanted for questioning in the death of her husband. No charges were pending against the woman yet, if she was still alive, but Rita should be detained and brought to Bergen County for an interview. Her husband was most likely dead, the victim of foul play. And the man caught disposing of the body had implicated Rita in the killing. The make and license of the Taurus Ilan had last seen his mother driving was attached to the alert. Rita Gluzman's BMW 530 remained in the driveway of the Upper Saddle River home. While still curious about her role, if any, in the death of her husband, if that was indeed Yakov Gluzman at the morgue, the police were nonetheless concerned for Rita Gluzman's safety.

When the police and coroner were granted a search warrant in Hackensack, Mary Anne Clayton and Coleen McVeigh, accompanied by their county police escort, returned to the East Rutherford garage at 2 A.M. from the medical examiner's office in Paramus to begin the enormous task of sorting through the disaster bags and organizing and reassembling numerous pieces of human body that had lain untouched for fourteen hours. The two women collected the bags and delivered them to their offices on Ridgewood Street, where they would begin an autopsy in the morning.

Lou Valvo was thinking of going home to get some rest, knowing that this would be his busiest Monday since joining the DA's office five months earlier. Instead, Valvo drove to his office in New City, the government center of Rockland, where Colantonio and Stewart joined the DA shortly after, at 3 A.M. Down the street from the county offices, not even the late-night convenience store was open that early so the three men fired up a pot of coffee in the third floor suite of offices that was home to the Rockland district attorney and got to work. The week was beginning very early for them.

Two

The four-story Rockland County office building in New City, New York, was abuzz Monday at 9 A.M., particularly the third floor, which housed the district attorney and his staff. A sleepless Lou Valvo had been put in charge of the prosecution of Vladimir Zelenin, aided by Steve Colantonio, and the DA's work involved first getting through the mountain of paperwork from East Rutherford, Orangetown, and Upper Saddle River, organizing all the reports together in a time-line chart along with the transcript of Goldrick's nine-hour session with the suspect and the FBI interpreter. The numerous jurisdictions involved in the two-state investigation were already making the prosecutor's job less linear and potentially more complicated than most cases, but the FBI, observing because the crime most likely involved its perpetrators crossing state lines—if Zelenin's statement were to be believed—had agreed to help streamline communication between the various departments.

Both Valvo and Colantonio had seen Vladimir Zelenin personally the night before, then watched as the prisoner had been led away from the East Rutherford station house to the Bergen County jail in Hackensack. There the suspect would await transfer to Rockland, pending both final disposition of the second-degree murder charge against him in New Jersey and the extradition order Valvo was beginning to process.

Bergen County had turned the murder case over to Valvo because the crime had occurred in Pearl River and protocol required that Rockland prosecute the case. Bergen's DA had committed its office's full support and resources to the Rockland authorities. The adjacent counties had a long history of spirited cooperation, owing to their close proximity, so it was unlikely there would be bickering over the kinds of territorial issues in which law enforcement agencies often got involved. Solving and successfully prosecuting a dramatic murder case is the mantle upon which detectives and prosecutors alike build long careers.

Sergeant Tom Goldrick had grown up in Rockland. His father had been the county sheriff until retiring four years earlier, and the younger Goldrick had an excellent working knowledge of the villages and enjoyed good relations within both the jurisdictions and the county's law agencies. Goldrick had in fact begun his career working for the New York State Attorney General on a special task force uncovering nursing home abuses in the late 1970s. In 1983 he'd been hired by the Bergen DA's office after the New York task force was disbanded. Following a year of general criminal work at BCI, the prestigious countywide detective force, Goldrick had become one of the eight homicide investigators reporting directly to the DA and was involved in dozens

of cases each year requiring intensive investigation in
the diverse New Jersey county.

Lou Valvo, meanwhile, was in the process of moving
to Rockland from Bergen County, near the Gluzman
home, where he lived before accepting an offer the
previous fall to be a trial lieutenant to newly elected
Rockland DA Michael Bongiorno, who now gave Valvo
free rein to lead the murder investigation.

As Colantonio sought search warrants for the Pearl
River apartment, the Bergen detectives visited ECI Technologies in East Rutherford and Rita and Yakov Gluzman's home for evidence of any kind that would either
substantiate or refute Zelenin's story.

In Paramus, Dr. Mary Anne Clayton advised her boss,
Dr. Sunandan B. Singh, of the progress her staff at the
Bergen medical examiner's office was making as they
began to log the numerous pieces of the body from the
garbage bags. Clayton, who with her staff performed
300 autopsies a year, had never had to reassemble a
decedent before. The morticians laid out the organs,
limbs, and head of what struck the coroner as a muscu-
lar, well-developed man, with little fat prior to his dismemberment. The technicians found a set of teeth
intact with the jaw in the same bag as the other parts,
surprising Clayton as a stupendous oversight by the
killer if he or she had gone to the trouble of removing
the fingerprints of the victim's hands to obscure his
identity. Clayton and her assistants had found the fingertip shavings as well in the garbage bags, and her staff
started matching them with the fingers. Like pieces of
a puzzle, the stiff, jagged fingertips fit in place on the
man's cold, lifeless hands. Two observations of Clayton's
became clearer as the day and the autopsy progressed:

the sixty-eight pieces of bone, organ, face, and flesh laying on the stainless steel tables in the medical examiner's workroom belonged to just one person. And whoever had performed the dissection had accurately cut the heart, lungs, and intestines with surgical precision, likewise the victim's limbs.

Fortunately, the skull was in one piece so that when the lips and nose recovered by the sheriff's divers were placed on its facial area, the completed face could be photographed and compared to possible victims by the doctors and detectives, though visual identification would not satisfy the requirement of proof to execute a death certificate. Clayton made an impression of the teeth while she waited for the dental records of Yakov Gluzman, who had not reported for work Monday at Lederle Laboratories. Gluzman had had some work done on his mouth using the company's dental plan, and his employer was able to process a set of the biologist's x-rays for comparison with the teeth at Bergen.

Zelenin's statement was appearing to be true in regard to the victim whose body he'd been caught dumping. It remained to be learned whether the Russian's other statements to Goldrick about his accomplice in the savage crime were as honest.

Monday afternoon Colantonio, Tom Hoffmann, and Valvo gathered around the New City office to discuss the variables of their investigation while they waited for a positive identification from Clayton of their victim. Each assumed it would be Yakov Gluzman. All were ready to proceed in the investigation into the killing and clinical evisceration of the scientist, whom they'd learned earlier was a cancer researcher prominent in scientific circles both in the U.S. and in Israel, where his parents and brother lived. There wasn't yet any sign of Rita Gluzman, who had not reported to her office at the Madison business park Monday morning and hadn't notified either Ilan or her employees, who included Rita's sister and mother, of her whereabouts.

The crime scene unit of the Rockland Sheriff's Department, working with Stewart and Colantonio's major case squad, had finished dusting Yakov Gluzman's apartment for fingerprints and other evidence. The criminalists hadn't found much out of the ordinary, other than the tiny trail of blood outside the front door. Inside, the apartment was spotless. The investigators had dusted the bathtub, where Zelenin had told Goldrick he and Rita Gluzman had dissected her husband's body two days earlier and, while there was some dried blood in the bathroom, it wasn't a great deal more than would have been expected under normal circumstances, such as the residue from a nasty cut on a finger or even a stubbed toe. It was almost fastidiously clean inside the two-room flat, the detectives observed. They would have to wait for the results of the blood tests and fingerprints. Perhaps there would be something useful to the investigation.

In the hallway leading from the bathroom to the living room, the detectives found little evidence suggesting to them that a struggle had occurred recently; there was no blood on the living room carpet, and the detectives were amazed that such a brutal murder could have happened there such a short time ago. But there was little debate among them that one had. Whoever had cleaned up the apartment had forgotten to clean outside in the hallway and the still-fresh stains led prominently downstairs to the first floor exit.

The Orangetown detectives, led by Tom Hoffmann, had found a witness, though one who'd seen the getaway of the probable killers, not the crime itself. Hoffmann had interviewed the couple who lived next door to Yakov

Gluzman: a retired New York City police officer and his wife. Early Sunday morning they had been awakened by the sound of a car alarm in the rear of the Celia Gardens complex. Looking out her second floor window the woman had seen a man and a woman run toward a blue car, close its trunk, and hurriedly drive off. It had taken several minutes before the car's driver disabled the annoying alarm, which stopped as he and his passenger drove away. At first the neighbor had thought it was an ordinary alarm malfunction, but upon hearing the news of Yakov Gluzman's death she wondered if there was a connection to the disturbance.

When did you see them? Hoffmann asked her. It was around 7 A.M. Sunday, Easter morning, the woman told the detective. And it had definitely been a man and a woman, the neighbor was certain.

The facts of Yakov Gluzman's life began to accumulate as the detectives interviewed co-workers at Lederle Laboratories, questioned Ilan Gluzman further about the nature of his parents' relationship, and looked through the personal belongings at the Celia Gardens apartment. Colantonio and Valvo learned that, among other things, friends of Yakov Gluzman had called him "Yasha." He was forty-eight years old, and a naturalized citizen of the U.S., where he had emigrated in 1977 with Rita and Ilan from Israel. Gluzman had earned a doctorate from the prestigious Weizmann Institute in Tel Aviv and begun a career as a biologist. He was popular with his co-workers, who said Gluzman had devoted his life to finding a cure for cancer.

In Upper Saddle River, BCI's detectives were searching the Gluzman residence thoroughly, looking through every corner of the 5,000-square-foot house for clues. Carlos Rodriguez was inspecting the garage, taking apart each crevice in the meticulously organized carport and

laundry area, when he loosened the airduct connecting
the clothes dryer to the wall. That's when the veteran
homicide detective spotted the business cards. They fell
out of the pipe, and had been inside of it. Odd, he
thought. Rodriguez took a closer look at the cards. One
of them belonged to a private investigator named Joe
Mullen, and had a New York City address, and on the
reverse of Mullen's business card the name "Mike" was
handwritten with a phone number in the 718 area code,
which placed it in one of four New York City boroughs
outside of Manhattan which shared the code. Rodriguez
catalogued the card, and mentioned it later to Colantonio. Perhaps it was something, perhaps not, thought
Rodriguez. In any case, it seemed quite unlike the owner
of this home to have anything out of order, even in the
laundry room. The detective noted that the home was
otherwise clean and immaculate.

Late Monday afternoon Mary Anne Clayton first tele-
phoned Goldrick, then Valvo. The body in her morgue
was indeed that of Yakov Gluzman, she said. The cohe-
sive set of body parts had been identified positively by
dental records; the fingerprints were being processed
and would take longer to confirm. It would take another
day or two to complete the autopsy, but the coroner
told Valvo that the victim's death had most likely been
caused by a severe blow to his forehead and skull area,
undoubtedly by an instrument such as an ax or a hatchet.

Three

Rockland County, at 276 square miles the smallest of New York's sixty-two counties except for the five boroughs of New York City, is twenty miles northwest of Manhattan and connected by numerous roads at its south end to Bergen County. Until the mid 1950s, Rockland consisted of family farms, small agrarian-oriented businesses, and was a weekend retreat for some of Manhattan's wealthy, most famously actress Helen Hayes. When the state's engineers built the Tappan Zee Bridge across the Hudson River in 1955, linking Rockland with affluent Westchester County to the east, the makeup of the county began to change. Rockland became another bedroom suburb of New York City and began to attract commuters, thanks to the Tappan Zee's access to passenger trains south to Grand Central Station and to the completion of the Palisades Interstate Parkway, which connected Rockland from Stony Point, near the U.S. Military Academy, south to New Jersey and the George

Washington Bridge. With housing prices less expensive than either Westchester or Nassau County on Long Island, Rockland became an attractive place to live, not quite as dense and more remote than either Nassau or Westchester, which are directly adjacent to New York City and accessible by public rail transportation. Families from the Bronx and Manhattan looking for a break from the congestion of the city filled housing developments in Nanuet, Nyack, and New City. Pearl River, a quaint village in southern Rockland, where Yakov lived and worked, became home to many New York City firefighters and police officers, a convenient commute to city precincts and within the means of civil servants while satisfying New York City's residency requirement that employees live in the state of New York.

By the 1990s, the sleepy county that was home to small farmers in the '50s had seen its population explode to 280,000 people. In 1996, construction began on the second-largest shopping mall in the United States, the two-million-square-foot Palisades Center on New York Route 59, the county's main east-west highway, in West Nyack.

Another dynamic had accompanied the growth of Rockland County and Orange County, to the west. A growing number of Orthodox Jews were leaving Brooklyn's Crown Heights and Williamsburg neighborhoods in order to raise their families in spacious, and politically and socially homogenous areas in the suburbs, such as Monsey, several miles west of Pearl River. They developed a formidable political base. The county's popular district attorney for twenty years, Kenneth Gribetz, was himself an observant Jew whose secular appearance (clean-shaven) and wardrobe (Brooks Brothers suit and tie) had been okayed by a rabbinical waiver of traditional orthodox dress and grooming codes, owing to the nature of his elective position and a respect for separation of church-and-state by Gribetz and his congregation.

When Gribetz, who had been frequently rumored as a candidate for attorney general or governor of New York during his tenure in Rockland, resigned as DA in May 1995, there suddenly was an opening for district attorney. Rockland's regular election was scheduled for November, but the county executive needed an interim DA to run the prosecutor's office. A number of lawyers throughout the county lobbied the supervisors for the position, which carried with it not only prestige but proximity to the seat of power in New York State, even if it was smaller than Westchester's or any of the five New York City DA's offices.

A young lawyer who lived in New City and thought of applying for the job had simply sent the board his résumé, dropping it in the mail with little fanfare and no lobbying effort. County executive C. Scott Vanderhoef liked what he read in the letter about the applicant's background as a prosecutor and called him for a formal interview. Two weeks later, on May 26, 1995, with the recommendation of Vanderhoef and the county's Republican Party leaders, New York Governor George Pataki appointed Michael Bongiorno, a top assistant to Manhattan DA Robert Morgenthau and a longtime Rockland resident to be the eighth district attorney in Rockland County's 100 years.

Bongiorno had grown up in Spring Valley, a small village between Nanuet and Monsey, when his family moved from the Bronx in the early 1960s. After graduating from Spring Valley High School in 1974, he'd been accepted to Yale, working his way through the exclusive Ivy League university with some financial aid and a campus job. The young Bongiorno had excelled in government and international law. His father had been a New York City police sergeant, providing his son with a thorough and unvarnished glimpse early on of the law enforcement world.

After graduating magna cum laude from Washington and Lee Law School in Virginia, Bongiorno returned to New York, where he was hired as an assistant DA in Morgenthau's criminal division, the spawning ground of prosecutors, defense attorneys, and judges in New York. Over the next fourteen years the quiet prosecutor had risen through the office to become a deputy Bureau chief of the trial division and one of Morgenthau's trusted assistants, charged with running a division of sixty assistant DAs prosecuting major cases in the nation's busiest and most famous district attorney's office. Vanderhoef and other of Rockland's trustees sensed he'd be more than capable of the task of running the county's justice operations.

Establishing himself in office quickly, Bongiorno won the office on his own six months later with fifty-three percent of the vote in the November election. Replacing a twenty-year incumbent is no easy task, but Bongiorno started by bringing in as his chief trial assistant his longtime friend Lou Valvo, also an alumnus of Morgenthau's office and someone Bongiorno had known and trusted since the early '80s, when Valvo was a legal assistant to Bongiorno while working his way through New York Law School. Valvo, like Bongiorno, preferred the fulfillment of public service, and both had forsaken more lucrative careers in private practice. The upbeat Valvo presented a good contrast to his boss: Bongiorno was a serious, studious public administrator; Valvo was an upbeat spirit with an easy laugh and quick sense of humor who proved to be the perfect front man for the office. After his 1995 election Bongiorno had convinced Valvo to leave his comfortable job in private practice, and its boredom in representing insurance companies, and move to Rockland, with its opportunity to do the work each knew as his calling.

Once Bongiorno had won a full four-year term, the DA identified the pressing problems facing Rockland County and the proactive manner in which his office would attack crime. The drug crisis affected the suburbs as much as it did the city, threatening the well-being of school children in New City and Nanuet as much as the sale of crack cocaine affected Brooklyn and Manhattan. Working with the local police departments, Bongiorno sought to identify and prosecute drug dealers in the five towns within his jurisdiction.

The second major issue the DA highlighted was one common throughout the U.S., and Bongiorno had taken pains to publicize the problem: domestic abuse.

On Tuesday morning Mike Bongiorno was facing his biggest challenge since taking office ten months before. The DA had a murder in his jurisdiction and a suspect in custody in New Jersey, and the suspect had quickly confessed and fingered an accomplice to the police. The implicated accomplice, who lived in New Jersey, was nowhere to be found. Bongiorno's case could not begin until the body parts had been identified and Vladimir Zelenin was extradited to New York. Now that he knew the victim was Yakov Gluzman, the DA couldn't rest until more evidence was found and any others involved in the murder of the scientist had been arrested, whether it had been Zelenin acting with another accomplice, or if his statement that Rita Gluzman had both inspired and aided him in the killing of her husband was true. The case wouldn't make progress, though, until Mrs. Gluzman was found, hopefully alive, and the investigators were able to question the woman about her whereabouts the evening of Saturday the 6th, when a witness claimed to have joined her in killing her husband, and about her subsequent disappearance Easter Sunday, when the police found the remains of her husband's body.

There had been no sightings of Rita Gluzman in more than two days, though security officials at the region's transportation outlets were still on alert and the local newspapers throughout the tri-state area of Connecticut, New Jersey, and New York had each carried the missing Mrs. Gluzman's photograph with the gruesome news stories of the butchery that had befallen somebody presumed to be her husband the day before.

Among the complexities of felony law in New York are the statutes governing murder, and Bongiorno and his staff understood the intricacies of them with exactness. While it can be classified as many things, murder is usually the premeditated, non-defensive, gratuitous taking of human life by another person. Whoever had killed Yakov Gluzman certainly appeared to fit the description of someone who had murdered. Legally, however, the crime's definition is more precise. In the Empire State, punishment for murder varies, depending on the circumstances of the killing.

New York had just reinstated its death penalty in 1995, following the election the year before of George Pataki as governor. Pataki had as a major plank of his platform a resumption of capital punishment, which three of the state's previous four governors had adamantly opposed, most notably Mario Cuomo, Pataki's predecessor. After the legislature in Albany passed the bill reinstating capital punishment and the governor signed it into law, statutes were revised to update sentencing guidelines for various capital crimes now that execution was a possibility. A result was a possible death sentence for several specific categories of murder and life imprisonment (or less) for other specific categories. It was the prerogative of local prosecutors to use the death penalty, and district attorneys throughout the state sought interpretations of the new law, some debating matters of personal conscience in deciding to use the ultimate punishment within their jurisdiction.

Mike Bongiorno had no personal problem in using the death penalty appropriately; he was in fact an advocate of its use, believing it to be effective in punishing violent criminals such as murderers while allowing the citizens of Rockland County to feel that justice had been done and some rightful retribution had been exacted for a wrongful act.

As Bongiorno reviewed the case, the prospect of a capital punishment case reaching Rockland's court seemed remote to the DA and his staff. First, Vladimir Zelenin had confessed to murdering Yakov Gluzman to the Bergen detectives and offered no resistance to being prosecuted in New Jersey or, after his extradition, in New York. Unknowingly, the admitted murderer, by pleading guilty to the barbaric act, had ironically been exempted from capital prosecution in New York or New Jersey if it could be proved to be first-degree murder. But Zelenin could be charged only with second-degree murder, not first, unless it could be proved he was in the process of committing another state felony when he killed Yakov Gluzman.

Zelenin's claim to have killed Gluzman only at the

insistence of Rita, under extreme duress, suggested to the prosecutors in both counties that the prisoner might have more to offer the justice system by his testimony against whoever had assisted him in the killing. But proving the case against an accomplice would be tough even with Zelenin's cooperation, until there was corroborating physical and circumstantial evidence that supported the man's story. Especially in state court in New York; the law made it impossible to charge or convict anyone of a felony based solely on the testimony of his or her accomplice. Bongiorno would have to wait until Rita Gluzman surfaced.

Steve Colantonio, the smooth twelve-year veteran of the DA's office and former U.S. Marshal, who the DA and Jim Stewart decided should spearhead the investigation with Orangetown detective Tom Hoffmann, met with Valvo Tuesday afternoon. They again sorted through reports from field investigators and summarized their findings: a murder had happened in Pearl River, there was a Russian-speaking suspect in custody. Both the victim and his missing wife had been born overseas, had relatives in Israel, and communicated in Hebrew and English. The three men nodded their heads in agreement. "Guess we should call Jake."

Deputy Sheriff Jacob Szpicek was known to all in the Rockland County police establishment as well as the Village of Monsey simply as Jake, even to those who could pronounce *shpeet-sek*. Born in the Warsaw Jewish Lodz ghetto in 1940, Jake Szpicek had known, for the first five years of his life, only his mother and the Catholic nuns with whom she had hidden him during World War II after the Nazis had killed his father and all their other male relatives. After the war his mother and he had emigrated to Palestine, where Jake joined the Israeli army in 1958, serving the mandatory four years before his wanderlust, and the attraction of the United States, led him to New York City. A year later, he settled in Nyack, married, and established a comfortable appliance repair business in Monsey. But his early ambition to do police work and public service ate at him constantly. Jake became an auxiliary cop, but even with his military service record age requirements in effect at the time prevented him from finding a regular police job. Then in the late '70s, as he approached forty, Jake had caught the attention of Ken Gribetz, who realized the value of having a dedicated cop around the county who spoke Hebrew. Gribetz knew a way around the age restriction, and the DA persuaded the Rockland sheriff to appoint Jake a part-time deputy. Suddenly, the county had a street cop to whom the growing Jewish population could relate. Jake's acumen and suggestions had benefited the police establishment on more than one occasion. It didn't hurt that he was fluent in five languages, including Hebrew and Yiddish, and had prominent contacts in Israel. As one longtime observer of Rockland law had put it, "There were more than enough guys around the police departments in the county who spoke Irish, you know? It kind of made sense to have someone around who spoke Jewish."

Valvo's team for the murder investigation was complete. All that was missing was Vladimir Zelenin, who through his public defender lawyer said he wouldn't fight extradition. And Rita Gluzman, who remained a mystery.

Four

The newspapers throughout the New York area played the story prominently. The killing of Dr. Yakov Gluzman was sensational, a shocking, major news event. In the *Bergen Record*, the major daily newspaper of northern New Jersey, four-color pictures and two lengthy articles adorned page one. *The New York Times* carried the story on the front of its Metro section, where major crimes committed in the New York area are splashed. The wire services ran the story wide and it was picked up in newspapers in Israel, Russia, and throughout Europe. In Rockland County, the local Gannett paper, the *Journal-News*, revealed that the county had its most gruesome crime in years.

The Gluzmans had been in the middle of a hotly contested divorce initiated by Yakov, and the Bergen detectives had found and interviewed the couple's lawyers. Yakov and Rita Gluzman had accumulated a fortune estimated at one and a half million dollars, and

Yakov had made a settlement offer to Rita in late 1995 that would have given her more than half that amount if she had agreed to the divorce. He had taken the Pearl River flat in early 1995, and the two had been formally separated for sixteen months when Yakov was killed.

Sightings of Rita Gluzman's blue 1995 Ford Taurus were starting to come in to Lou Valvo's office. The nationwide alert was showing results after only a day and a half, remarkable when considering the amount of traffic in the New York area. At LaGuardia airport, Rita's Taurus had been recorded entering the long-term parking lot at 3 P.M. Sunday afternoon. The car passed through the LaGuardia exit two hours later, evidently not using the long-term facility. Then a routine license-run by a patrol officer in Baldwin, Long Island, Sunday night had come up with the Taurus' license. There hadn't been cause to pull over the car, the Baldwin police said, though occasional checks of out-of-state plates, even those from neighboring New Jersey, were common. Unfortunately, Valvo's alert hadn't gotten over the wire until early Monday morning. But together, the two sightings reported to the DA Tuesday afternoon helped him narrow Rita's range. The only way to drive off Long Island is by ferry, or back through New York City.

It remained to be learned whether Rita Gluzman had been driving the Taurus when it was sighted, or if she too had fallen victim to foul play.

"She isn't a suspect yet," Valvo told reporters. "We only want her for questioning."

Armed with the search warrant granted in Rockland, Jake Szpicek almost immediately had begun combing through Yakov Gluzman's phone records from the Pearl River apartment. Most of the hundreds of long distance calls the deputy found had been to Israel, so Szpicek began dialing each of the numbers in Hadera, Tel Aviv, and Jerusalem, waiting for someone to pick up. The number would answer, and Szpicek would ask in Hebrew whether the party knew Yasha, then about what sort of relationship he or she had had. Yakov Gluzman's killing had been big news in Israel, so by the end of his calling task whoever answered had heard of the doctor's demise already. When Szpicek identified himself as a local American cop trying to solve the murder case, he'd been able to mention the names of several prominent Israeli police commanders in case the person at the other end had any doubts of Szpicek's identity. "If you have any questions, sir, just talk with Superintendent Tzubery, the chief of Hadera police. He and I were on *kibbutz* together." That had been enough for most to loosen up to the caller. Szpicek started compiling a list of Yasha's associates: who was business, who was family, and who was in some other category. He looked for clues that might explain why the killer or killers had cut Yakov Gluzman up so viciously.

One number in Israel that had showed up repeatedly had no answering machine, and kept ringing through without an answer. Szpicek kept trying the number, and finally, a woman's voice answered.

"Hello?"

"This is Deputy Sheriff Jacob Szpicek calling from the United States, from New York. Sorry much to bother you, miss, but were you friend of Yasha Gluzman?"

Silence.

"Please, I am a sheriff investigator in Rockland County, where Yasha's apartment is. I need your help in finding who did this unspeakable thing to Yakov Gluzman. General Hefetz will guarantee your safety. Call him and tell him you spoke with Jake Szpicek. He will reassure you. Please help."

After a minute, the woman broke her silence. "This has been a nightmare! Yasha is dead. They're going to blame me!" the woman cried.

Szpicek had felt more than a little elation upon hearing the woman's reaction. He just might have found the lead he was looking for.

The 580-acre campus of Lederle Laboratories in Pearl River extends more than a mile west of the intersection of Middletown Road and New York Route 304, about a mile north of the New Jersey border, nineteen miles from midtown Manhattan, in a lot that was originally a dairy farm before Ernest Lederle, the pharmaceutical giant's founder, presciently picked up the first forty-acre lot for $4,500 in 1906. Lederle, who had been Health Commissioner of New York City, had set out to find a cure for diphtheria, the fatal ailment he'd witnessed too much of during the great wave of European immigration from 1885 to the turn of the twentieth century. Within seven years, Lederle introduced a cure that would reduce the mortality rate in children as a result of diphtheria from an astronomic forty percent to a near-minuscule four percent in thirty years. Lederle sold his company to American Cyanamid in 1930, and the chemical company continued the doctor's work. Now one of Rockland County's largest employers, 2,800 scientists, manufacturing personnel, clerks, and others work at the Lederle campus, and 28,000 annual visitors keep its thirty acres of parking lot filled. It was at the Pearl River lab that the first oral polio vaccine was manufactured beginning in the 1950s, and after its acquisition by American Home Products in 1994, Lederle was made part of the packaged goods conglomerate's Wyeth Ayerst division. Today approximately forty percent of all generic prescription drugs used in the U.S. emanate from the Rockland campus.

Yakov Gluzman had gone to work at Lederle in 1987, after spending ten years in residence as a biologist at Cold Spring Harbor Laboratories on Long Island, where he made his name in the United States. Working with Dr. James Watson, the Nobel Laureate who had explained genetic components, Gluzman had worked on a team that discovered a particular cell used to identify cancer, shortcutting the time required to attack the disease. This had catapulted him into the sphere of first-rank cancer researchers in the U.S., and he left to continue his cancer work and develop new drugs to fight that and other life-threatening illnesses. The management at Lederle had been more than impressed both with Gluzman's work at Cold Spring Harbor and his life's devotion to medicine. He had become a master biologist, one of the quietly prominent souls in research whose effect is felt anonymously at the pharmacy counter. By 1995, after eight years at Lederle, Gluzman had risen to a senior research position and was earning $170,000 a year, with generous benefits. Lederle had given the scientist an open checkbook to continue his biomedical research. He was, for lack of a more formal title, the chief of the biology division at Lederle.

With additional income Rita took as a draw from ECI, the couple's company, the Gluzmans could easily afford the $4,500 monthly mortgage and upkeep on their Upper Saddle River home. Otherwise, the detectives found, Yakov lived with little ostentation, preferring to drive the eight-year-old Maxima. A big night out might be dinner at Sammy's Rumanian in Manhattan, the dining mecca for upper-middle-class Jews in New York who longed for a European meal. No slave to fashion, Gluzman spent modestly on his wardrobe while keeping

up a good appearance. He'd been able to send his
parents some money, and when he left the New Jersey
home, Yakov had found the bachelor apartment on
Middletown Road three blocks from Lederle in an
unprepossessing complex of forty-year-old two-story
brick buildings. Gluzman respected his money and,
while not frugal, managed it well. Unlike Rita, who they
learned was more extravagant, Yakov was down-to-earth
and unpretentious. Only Rita Gluzman's desire to live
in a fashionable part of northern New Jersey, in fact, had
taken them to the upscale New Jersey suburb instead of
another, less expensive village near Lederle, in New
York.

Yakov Gluzman was not the average murder victim
in America by any statistical standard. The more they
learned about him, the more the detectives and the DA
came to look with disgust on his killers. By midweek,
it had become clear somebody had assisted Vladimir
Zelenin, between the sighting of two people leaving
Celia Gardens early Sunday and the improbability of
Zelenin having driven both his Taurus and Yakov's Maxima to One Madison alone, with Yakov's body in both
cars.

Ilan Gluzman had been born in Israel in 1971, though
under different circumstances than most children that
year: his father was detained indefinitely in his native
Soviet Union while Rita had emigrated with her parents
the previous year, promising before she left to do everything possible to gain Yakov, her new husband, a safe
exit to Tel Aviv with her. After their reunion in Israel,
Rita Gluzman had attended the Weizmann Institute,
too, and was educated there as a chemist.

The Soviet government hadn't wanted Yakov Gluzman to leave Moscow, where the young man had shown great promise as an undergraduate science major at Moscow State University. Though the Soviet Union was hostile to Jews, promising scientists who could help the then-Communist nation in its defense industry were discouraged from leaving. The postwar "brain drain" had had a significant effect on eastern Europe, especially Russia, East Germany, and the other former Iron Curtain countries by the flight to the United States of the brightest and most talented scientists, who were skeptical of living in the totalitarian dictatorship that was the Soviet Union. Yakov Gluzman, born in the Ukraine, had more to offer his country than it wanted to lose by his emigration to Israel.

Rita had demonstrated at the United Nations in her effort to get Yakov freed, at one point conducting an eighteen-day hunger strike on the steps of the international peace organization to gain attention to her husband's plight. Her fast had worked, and Yakov had been issued an exit visa to Israel, where he met his infant son Ilan.

Vladimir Zelenin had gotten some sleep in his cell at the Bergen County jail in the days since his apprehension in East Rutherford, and had begun talking again to Goldrick. The prisoner was still unsure whether he would cooperate with the government, but Goldrick continued to listen with interest to the prisoner's story.

Rita had threatened to evict him and his young sons from the Fair Lawn apartment ECI provided for him if he didn't go along with her plan to kill Yakov Gluzman, Zelenin said. He made eight dollars an hour working at his cousin's company as a handyman, and Rita had loaned him one of the company's older Tauruses for transportation. He had no money saved; it was impossible to sustain the family without the apartment subsidy. And his political asylum was still in process; he had no green card and therefore limited mobility in a country in which he barely could communicate. He could still be deported, back to Kyrgyzstan, where most surely he and his sons would be tormented or killed. That's why it had been so easy for Rita to coerce him into the crime, the man said. He existed at her whim. Even in Kyrgyzstan, where he'd earned a master's degree in physics, he'd been able to find work only as a janitor. He'd taught for a while, but the region's anti-Semitic establishment had made life difficult, he continued.

Goldrick and BCI had executed a search warrant at the Zelenin apartment in Fair Lawn, and whatever evidence found there would be logged with the prisoner's statement.

Under New Jersey law, because Vladimir Zelenin had been arrested and charged with a Class A felony in the Garden State, he continued to be held at the Hackensack jail, although it was assumed he would eventually be transferred to Rockland for prosecution in New York state, where a more serious murder charge could be entered against him. Bergen could prosecute Zelenin for second-degree murder, as the man had confessed to the killing, but the extent of his provable crime in New Jersey absent his confession had been disposing of the body parts. After he was safely in the New City jail, he could repeat his statement to Valvo and the Rockland court, while the detectives determined who had been with the man the night of the murder.

By early Thursday, there had been no new sightings of Rita Gluzman or her car. She hadn't boarded any international flights, at least not using her own passport. And she hadn't used any of her credit cards since Saturday. The Rockland investigators had alerted the director's office at Cold Spring Harbor Laboratories to be on the lookout for Rita, whom the people there remembered from her days with Yakov at the prestigious campus overlooking Long Island Sound on the island's North Shore. The Nassau County Police were on the alert for Rita's blue Taurus and its New Jersey plate. Colantonio had found Rita's sister, Mariann Rabinovich, who also lived in Upper Saddle River.

Lou Valvo was by nature skeptical, especially of what appeared obvious. While he might light up a room with his smile, it was clear his mind worked overtime analyzing all that lay within his reach. He'd cut his teeth at the Manhattan DA's office, working for Bongiorno and Robert Morgenthau during the 1980s. Undecided on a career out of college, Valvo had gone to the DA's office as a paralegal where he met Bongiorno and was exposed to career prosecutors. He then had decided to go to law school and become one of them. Fifteen years watching criminals and hanging around courtrooms had given him invaluable insights into the minds of many bad guys. Zelenin was no different from many of the violent, desperate criminals Valvo had sent away in his career, despite his protestations. But the Russian's story was beginning to check out. After all, Valvo reasoned, if Rita Gluzman was alive, and had been at all awake the previous four days, surely she had heard of her husband's bloody killing and of Zelenin's capture by the police. Why hadn't Rita come forward in that time? After all, the police had the killer in custody, and were concerned for the safety of the victim's widow. Who was she hiding from? What about the timing of her disappearance? If she'd been pulling into the LaGuardia parking lot at 3 P.M. Sunday, then turned around and went elsewhere, where was she thinking of going, and why? Because at three Sunday afternoon, the DA knew, only a handful of people could have been aware that Yakov Gluzman was dead. Vladimir Zelenin was one. Tom Goldrick was another. Richard Freeman, too.

Only the person who had been Zelenin's accomplice could have possibly known that the bags of body parts Freeman had found with Zelenin belonged then to Yakov Gluzman. There'd been no identification of the victim over the radio or television.

Only Rita Gluzman, if she were alive, would be able to tell Lou Valvo why she'd suddenly taken off, abandoning her business and family unannounced, coincidentally the day after her estranged husband's murder.

Five

Friday, April 12, would turn out to be an eventful and important day in Lou Valvo's short tenure at the Rockland DA's office. That morning, the first assistant prosecutor began formal extradition procedures with Bergen County for Vladimir Zelenin, having won an indictment of the confessed killer from the Rockland grand jury on Thursday. Zelenin had told prosecutors in both counties that he wouldn't fight extradition to New York. Further, the man indicated his willingness to cooperate with the police investigation and as a witness against Rita Gluzman. With his transfer to New York State, all the physical evidence collected at One Madison from the Taurus and the Maxima, along with the results of Mary Anne Clayton's autopsy of the body parts, would be officially released to Rockland for use there by the prosecutors. Zelenin could be processed into the system, and his statement entered into the record, in New York State, where the investigation into the murder of Yakov

Gluzman was centered. A hearing was scheduled in Hackensack. Extradition was granted.

Then Valvo got a phone call from the police department in Laurel Hollow, New York, a small village on Long Island in Nassau County. Rita Gluzman had been found, and the woman was in their custody.

Famous throughout the science world, Cold Spring Harbor Laboratories is located at the border of Nassau and Suffolk Counties, the two large entities that comprise Long Island. Its eighty-acre center on the island's north shore overlooks a beautiful natural harbor, a pleasing environment for the laboratory's 200 full-time scientists, 150 post-graduate students, and 6,000 annual visitors to study cancer, neurobiology, and plant genetics as they strive to fulfill CSHL's mission of improving the human condition by fighting its most serious ailments. The Rockefeller Foundation had helped its endowment greatly, and its renowned president, Dr. James D. Watson, was awarded the Nobel Prize in medicine in 1962, when he had been one of the scientists who had discovered DNA structure. It was CSHL that had brought Yakov Gluzman to the United States in 1977, and the Gluzmans had lived in one of the many tidy cottages there for five years before buying a home nearby.

Gluzman's death had shocked Watson and Dr. Winship Herr, who had known the biologist intimately during his ten years there, when they'd identified the gene for shortcutting cancer treatment together. They too had wondered what had become of Rita in the days after the discovery of their friend's gruesomely dissected body fifty miles away in New Jersey.

During a routine check of the bungalows used to

house visitors, one of the housekeeping staff at Cold Spring had surprised a woman in an apartment that normally should have been vacant. The cleaning woman hadn't recognized the woman from a poster the Cold Spring administrators had circulated earlier in the week: but the stranger was Rita Gluzman. Rita then had climbed out the window of the first floor cottage to avoid the housekeeper, and was caught by a security guard in the faculty lunchroom and detained for trespassing. Rita had neglected to check in with the front office.

Because the authorities in Bergen and Rockland had notified Herr and the other administrators of their interest in interviewing Rita Gluzman, her discovery had been less of a social surprise than one for great concern by Herr's staff. Because she'd resisted, showing little sign of visiting Cold Spring to catch up with old acquaintances like Herr, the security director, Art Brings, called the local village police in Laurel Hollow, who came and arrested Rita. Brings and Officer Thomas Englemann had confronted Gluzman on the lunchroom patio where a group of visiting scientists were dining, confronting and then cuffing her for the short trip to the Second Precinct station house of the Nassau County Police Department in Woodbury. The cops found a number of maps, travel guides of Switzerland, some hair color, and several passports on Rita. Finding her car elsewhere on the sprawling campus, the Laurel Hollow police had processed its license plates, which were New York issue, and learned they had been reported stolen Monday in nearby Hicksville at a parking lot in a shopping mall there. Cataloging Rita's personal items found in the car, the police also discovered what to most would seem an unusual item to take along on casual travel: a set of Henckel knives.

The Nassau County police charged Rita Gluzman Friday afternoon with trespassing and possession of stolen property, holding her awaiting a hearing before the local magistrate. That evening, appearing at her arraignment as a throng of two hundred reporters and camera crew waited outside the village courthouse, Gluzman was informed that she'd continue to be held in custody in Nassau County. Telling Rita and her newly hired defense attorney, Michael Rosen, that this "was no ordinary burglary" and the possibility of murder charges against her existed elsewhere, Judge Claire Weinberg denied bail to the widow. The Nassau County Assistant DA had argued that Gluzman was a flight risk, owing to her disappearance after her husband's death, the stolen license plates, and the Swiss travel brochures found on her at the Cold Spring Harbor bungalow. Switzerland is a country with no extradition treaty with the U.S. Stealing the New York license plates, which Gluzman had admitted during her booking, added even more suspicion about her travel plans.

Valvo and Colantonio went to Long Island to interview Gluzman after the call from the Laurel Hollow PD. While claiming officially that she still wasn't a suspect, the two men had fewer reasons, after her five-day disappearance, to believe that her cousin, Zelenin, might be lying in his implication of her. In fact, Mike Bongiorno and Lou Valvo had stopped giving Rita Gluzman the benefit of any doubt they might have had about her complicity in her husband's brutal murder. After hearing from Hoffmann, Colantonio, and Jake Szpicek, they awaited the arrival of Zelenin and the crime scene evidence, which they could then begin to analyze in New City.

Under New York's laws concerning detainment, the

DA had six days to make his case if he planned to charge Rita with a felony or she would be freed. The Rockland DA wanted also to determine just *why* Rita Gluzman would have wanted Yakov dead.

Six

In the days since the discovery of the murder in their jurisdiction, Mike Bongiorno and Lou Valvo had challenged every assumption of the crime and analyzed each of its possible participants. While they continued a search for other suspects, their investigation team hadn't yet produced concrete proof of Rita's involvement, and there was only her cousin's sworn statement that she'd coerced him into killing Yakov. Though her fingerprints were most likely all over the furniture, appliances, and other areas of the Pearl River apartment, it was clear Gluzman had visited her husband's apartment on many occasions during their year-long separation and it was apparent the couple had continued their sexual relationship even as their divorce came closer to reality.

Other of Rita's actions, though, were being brought to light by the detectives' continuing legwork, and like pieces of a puzzle, these discoveries convinced the detec-

tives and prosecutors of the woman's active involvement
in the premeditated killing and subsequent dismemberment of Yakov Gluzman. Now that she was safely in
custody, resolving the reasons for her behavior and closing the murder case would be easier for the Rockland
task force.

One of the questions that had puzzled Bongiorno,
Valvo, and Colantonio throughout the week concerned
Vladimir Zelenin: why had he killed Yakov Gluzman?
There was no apparent reason for the Russian's actions
in murdering the scientist on his own. The detectives
couldn't see any possible financial gain in his killing
Gluzman. No business agreements seemed to exist
between the two men where much would be gained by
Gluzman's death. Zelenin, who had two teenage children to support by himself, barely scraped by on his $8
per hour job at ECI, managing to survive thanks to the
rent-free apartment Rita provided for him and his two
sons, along with the ten-year-old Taurus that had been
a company car. Zelenin's situation appeared unlikely to
change for the better with Gluzman out of the picture,
unless the man had been paid to kill his cousin's husband. The detectives were looking into whether somebody else might have hired Zelenin to kill Gluzman,
though there was no obvious enemy, rival, or other party
whom they could ascertain wanted the biologist dead.
The FBI agents were continuing to examine the possibility of a connection to the Russian mafia, but so far could
not find one.

It was Zelenin's pliancy with Sergeant Tom Goldrick
that astounded Steve Colantonio and Lou Valvo, though
each had come to his own conclusions about both the
veracity of the Russian's statements and the motivation
of Zelenin in coming forth to each of them so willingly.
Colantonio had thought upon first seeing Zelenin Eas-

ter Sunday night while the prisoner was being interrogated at East Rutherford by Goldrick that there was a sexual relationship between Zelenin and Rita Gluzman. Other than money, what else might have driven the Russian to kill Yakov Gluzman? The skeptical Colantonio had seen enough criminals and heard every explanation throughout his career, and his experience had taught the detective to begin with the basest of motives in determining the reason for a crime. Zelenin had shown the sort of tension Colantonio had seen in sexual relationships between criminal partners before. After a day or so, though, the detective had eliminated sex between the cousins as a possibility as it became clear to him there was none and that Rita had abandoned Zelenin as well as her other family members when she fled.

Contrition and guilt rarely needed translation from one language to another. Zelenin seemed to be communicating his remorse thoroughly to Colantonio and Valvo, who sensed genuine misgivings on their prisoner's part, not so much about being caught, but about killing someone who, it turned out, was one of a limited number of people who had helped the Kyrgyzstanian immigrant in his moments of deepest despair. It had also become obvious to Zelenin almost at once that Rita had abandoned him, leaving him to face the rest of his life in prison, or possibly an executioner, after he had done the treacherous job of killing her husband, simply so he could avoid being left destitute and reported to the immigration authorities by her. Zelenin's surrender and behavior since his arrest suggested to them that the man had abandoned any hope for his immediate future and gladly cooperated with the government in their pursuit of his Rita both because he felt betrayed by her and he had accepted and reconciled in his mind the imminent lengthy imprisonment awaiting him.

The detectives and Valvo had concluded that their prisoner's story was credible.

Zelenin's court-appointed public defender in Bergen County had had to postpone two formal extradition hearings owing to pressing serious cases at the Hackensack courthouse, and Valvo and Colantonio were dying to get both the prisoner and the collateral evidence to New City. Both the prosecutor and the detective's instincts had convinced them Rita Gluzman was involved.

The investigative team took a look at the lives of both Rita and Yakov Gluzman, and charted what they had learned about the couple.

The contested divorce in New Jersey involved an estate estimated at $1.5 million, which the Gluzmans had accumulated almost entirely since arriving from Israel nineteen years before. It included savings, pensions from both Cold Spring Harbor Labs and Lederle, the New Jersey home, their former home on Long Island near Cold Spring Harbor, and, of no minor significance either to Yasha or Rita, the family's electroplating company, ECI, which manufactured systems for computer keyboards. In the divorce, the major disagreement between the two centered on control of the eight-year-old business, which Yakov had financed with $300,000 of his savings. Rita ran the company as its chief executive.

Yakov's income from Lederle was sufficient to cover both the expenses of the Upper Saddle River home and his bachelor apartment in Pearl River. Rita had taken a salary of $50,000 from her work as president of ECI in 1995, and in response to Yakov's settlement offer the previous fall she'd claimed to need alimony from him in order to maintain the house and pay her ordinary monthly expenses, which included a personal trainer, frequent trips to a beauty salon, the upkeep of the BMW, and a therapist. As was the case with many small business entrepreneurs, Rita paid a number of her monthly obligations from ECI's general expense funds. The company, jointly owned by the two with sales of roughly $3 million in 1995, had earned a pre-tax profit that year of only $30,000 or so. It was after Yasha had filed for divorce that Rita stated to her husband's lawyer that the income she earned from running ECI, even combined with several hundred thousand dollars Yakov had offered her from his pension plans at Lederle and other assets such as the biologist's insurance policies, would not cover her anticipated expenses, some five or six thousand dollars monthly. Because Ilan Gluzman was an adult, he was considered an emancipated child, so support by either parent for the Gluzman son, who had begun a career as an engineer and worked at ECI, was not a consideration. Ilan lived at home with his mother.

During the settlement talks, Yasha had granted Rita his share of the Upper Saddle River home, which the detectives learned was worth roughly $500,000. Even with the equity the couple had accumulated in the property since buying it in 1989, when they'd moved from Long Island, the mortgage payment and taxes each month were too much for Rita to afford alone. She wanted majority ownership of ECI, which was becoming a cash-flow cow, and Rita and her lawyer pressed Yakov to relinquish his stock and give it to Rita in the settlement offer. This Yakov had refused to do, but he told them he would have little problem giving up a majority of ECI as long as Ilan was the recipient. Yakov had insisted, though, on seeing the company's books, which

Rita had not allowed him to do during their separation. He had suspected that the business he'd funded and from which he had yet to receive any profits or return of his capital had been cooking its books at Rita's direction.

Rita had hired Zelenin as a jack-of-all-trades helper. Many small family businesses operated similarly. ECI paid for their apartments and other expenses, too. But Yakov had suspected Rita was getting carried away by her spending habits and worried that his $300,000 investment establishing ECI would be lost forever, paying for Rita's luxuries.

The DA knew there were money disputes between Rita and Yakov Gluzman and their divorce had been stalled while the two straightened out the issue of ECI's books to Yasha's satisfaction. But every couple in the United States fought at some point over money, and Yakov Gluzman had offered Rita no serious obstacle to her walking from their marriage with nearly $800,000 in cash and property, more than half the couple's worth. And she'd refused his offer, which seemed on its surface to be generous.

Jake Szpicek reported to Colantonio and Valvo with what he'd discovered by his persistent phone-calling to Israel, Russia, and Europe, and there were suddenly additional reasons to suspect Rita. The sheriff's deputy had spoken with Michael Gluzman, Yakov's younger brother, who was grieving and angry at the loss of Yakov. Szpicek had reached a woman in Hadera, a city near Tel Aviv, who said she had known Yasha Gluzman intimately, and was distraught over the scientist's death. The woman, Raisa Korenblit, told Szpicek she had been seeing Yasha Gluzman romantically for more than a year. They had met during one of the scientist's frequent trips to Israel, not long after Yakov had separated from Rita and moved to Pearl River. In late 1995, the two had begun dating. She was in shock, devastated at the death of the man who was planning, she said, to move to Israel to be with her, once he could settle his divorce.

The detectives and DA talked it over: was this woman Korenblit the classic "other woman," some paramour who had overstated her relationship with a now-dead man to attach his assets? Was her story true about knowing Yakov intimately, about his desire to reunite with her in Israel? Szpicek had verified Korenblit's story with Michael Gluzman, Yakov's brother.

Yasha had taken Korenblit out socially with his brother and with their father, Chaim Gluzman, in Hadera. It was common knowledge within the family there that Yakov was leaving Rita and that he'd been smitten with the thirty-five-year-old Korenblit, an agriculturist. Neither Yasha's brother nor father had wanted necessarily to see the man's family break up, but they realized that Ilan had graduated from college and begun a career. There were no other considerations. If Yasha had decided in middle age after all that he'd done for his father, brother, wife, and son that he would change his life situation, so be it, they had agreed. Yasha had become a great success, more than any father had hoped for, the elder Gluzman had suggested, and Michael was an adoring brother who had greatly admired his older brother. It hadn't bothered Michael Gluzman that his brother was keeping the company of a woman other than Rita, either. He had observed too many unnecessary fights between Rita and Yakov through the years, and thought his sister-in-law to be abusive.

Michael Gluzman hadn't trusted Rita and thought of his sister-in-law as an angry woman who had been rarely satisfied with all that Yakov did for her and jealous that her husband was sending money to his family in Israel. He wasn't surprised at Rita's disappearance after his brother had been savagely killed. The younger Gluzman offered to come to the United States at any time to assist in prosecuting anyone responsible for the death of his brother.

The DA learned from the investigators that Rita had discovered Yasha's affair with Korenblit. Knowing about Yakov's liaison with the younger Korenblit had angered Rita, and she had expressed anxiety on more than one occasion to those around her at the thought of another woman entering her husband's life, even as she and Yakov were on course to end their marriage.

Worse, as far as Rita Gluzman's emotions were concerned, it turned out that Yakov had been a popular bachelor once he decided to leave Rita. There were other women the biologist had seen in the year since leaving Rita, and they, too, were devastated and afraid of Rita Gluzman.

But to Bongiorno, Valvo, and Colantonio the most blatant incriminating detail leading them to suspect Rita had been her flight. Rita told the Rockland detectives during her interview Friday in Nassau County that she'd fled because she thought somebody was trying to kill her, too, after they had killed Yakov. Her husband was dead, and she was frightened for her life. She had gone to Cold Spring Harbor because, she said, it was a former home where she knew she'd be safe, especially if an assassin was after her. She wasn't planning to leave the country, but didn't know whether some paid killer was out to get both Yasha and her. How could I trust the police anyway? she had inferred. What if they had been involved? The police in Russia were, all the time, the

Ukrainian told the cops and the DA. That's why she had fled Upper Saddle River, and hadn't called any authorities anywhere after learning of Yasha's death.

But the DAs again asked themselves the $64-question: if it couldn't have been known by anyone other than the killer or killers that Yasha Gluzman was dead until, at the earliest, Sunday night, after Sergeant Goldrick had recorded Zelenin's statement, why had Rita fled for LaGuardia airport early Sunday afternoon? Why had she gone to Cold Spring Harbor Sunday evening thinking her husband dead if there were no news reports stating the victim had been Yakov Gluzman?

Rita Gluzman could not explain that inconsistency.

And who other than Rita fit the profile of a suspect in the murder? There didn't appear to be many possible accomplices to Zelenin who would have had access to the handyman, convinced him to kill Yakov, and helped him gain access to his victim's apartment, which had shown no signs of forcible entry the night of the killing. Because they had ruled out Zelenin acting alone, the DAs were certain there was an accomplice.

So Mike Bongiorno and Lou Valvo had come to a conclusion: Rita Gluzman should be charged with murder, the premeditated kind, and be prosecuted for her role in the death of her husband. But it wouldn't be simple to either charge or convict their prime suspect. First, unless the prosecutors could suggest and prove another felony Rita had committed during the murder, such as burglary, robbery, or kidnapping, they could only press second-degree murder charges, and the maximum sentence in state court would be 25 to life. Premeditated murder on its own wouldn't qualify Yakov Gluzman's killing for the capital punishment possible with a first-degree murder conviction. Both Valvo and Bongiorno knew it would be tough to prove burglary, which would elevate the crime to first degree, because of Yakov's conjugal visits from Rita. She could probably prove she had a set of keys to his apartment and was a weclome guest, not a burglar. Further, under New York's strict codes, with only Zelenin's testimony in their arsenal of evidence to use in court, Rita might be acquitted. Worse, the case might likely be dismissed, and Rita would walk away a free—and wealthy—widow. But the diligent Bongiorno had done his homework. The prosecutors had another option open to them, thanks in part to the fight for midnight basketball in the nation's cities and to a president who had sought women's votes for reelection by showing them he understood their pain.

The headlines surrounding the investigation of the murder of Yakov Gluzman continued in New York and throughout the United States and the rest of the world. The case presented an opportunity for a prosecutor to make his or her career, particularly if one had ambitions that carried beyond the local courthouse. If the Rockland DA brought Rita Gluzman to trial, the sensational nature of the crime and characters would surely bring CNN and Court TV to the New City courthouse and the face of the prosecutor to viewers of the nightly news on the other major networks. The constant glare of television cameras, combined with the usual throng of reporters and news media who would be expected to cover a murder trial with international importance, could lead to the sort of fame that was the dream of district attorneys elsewhere in America nearly every day of their working lives. But the trial might well produce an ulcer, too, for everyone involved, if the government were to lose an otherwise convincing case in state court simply because of evidentiary problems. Bongiorno had learned from his years with Morgenthau to avoid the spectacle of trials that had a potential downside, where a normally open-and-shut case might be lost, embarrassingly as well as expensively, because the prosecutor hadn't paid attention to the rule of law.

So the DA had examined other possibilities in bringing justice to the killers of Yakov Gluzman. Bongiorno knew that Zelenin's hearing at the Rockland courthouse would be a simple affair, with the judge there entering the man's plea to the crime and setting a sentencing date. There would be little trial expense to the Rockland taxpayers, and Zelenin's uncontested guilty plea substantiated by his capture with the victim's body was all the DA would need to quickly convict the man of Yakov Gluzman's murder.

The downside of Rockland's prosecuting the case against Rita Gluzman was the possibility of Zelenin's accomplice walking away while costing county taxpayers an enormous sum. Analyzing necessary DNA evidence alone, for example, would be a major expense. The lab charged $500 to test each sample of blood to determine whose it might be. The detectives had collected hundreds of samples from the Pearl River apartment and East Rutherford that would be crucial to prove the case against Rita in court, if they charged her, so off the top perhaps half a million dollars would be spent to deliver potentially incriminating blood samples to a jury that might not even consider them useful. Bongiorno's budget for DNA testing for all of 1996 was only $50,000. Valvo added up the expense of a trial, and had concluded it would be roughly a million dollars, or approximately one-fifth of the total operating budget of the Rockland DA's office. And for what? Rita would most 'ikely win acquittal, unless the detectives found other direct evidence that could be introduced in state court to prove she had killed her husband.

During the days before Rita's arrest Bongiorno had called across the Hudson River to White Plains, to the U.S. Attorney's Southern District satellite office on Quarropas Street, which prosecuted crimes at the federal level in the six counties north of New York City. The DA and Deirdre Daly, the U.S. Attorney's deputy in charge of the Westchester County office, spoke about the federal implications of Yakov Gluzman's murder. Because the crime had occurred in two states, any number of U.S. laws were applicable in pursuing its perpetrators. The case had Daly's complete attention, especially since the FBI had become involved.

Daly called in one of her assistant U.S. attorneys, Cathy Seibel, who also had reviewed the case that week. It seemed like a local murder case, and there was no federal murder statute, Seibel had offered, but there were other federal laws, certainly, that might be used in an interstate case involving a heinous killing. Daly and Seibel told Bongiorno and Valvo that if there was any way the U.S. Attorney's Office might help Rockland's prosecution to call at any time and they would look at appropriate laws covering conspiracies to murder.

Crucial to their discussions, the DA and the U.S. Attorney knew that under federal evidence guidelines, which differed in many ways from those of the states, the testimony of an accomplice, used with other circumstantial evidence, was satisfactory both to indict and convict a suspect. Without those enlightened evidence rules, high-level drug dealers, kidnappers, and white-collar criminals would be immune from prosecution.

Now that Rita Gluzman was in custody on Long Island, six days remained under New York State law to either charge the widow with a felony or provide for bail on the trespassing and possession of stolen property charges that had landed her in jail in the first place. Rita could afford almost any bail amount set, even if it were a million dollars. So Bongiorno knew he had to act quickly, but correctly, and the DA told Daly and Seibel he and his office would get back to them as soon as possible once the lab results and detectives' reports were complete, and when he decided which route his prosecution of Rita Gluzman, if there were any, might take.

Seven

Late on Friday the 12th, Rita Gluzman's newly hired attorney, Mike Rosen, a top-shelf criminal trial lawyer from New York City retained on her behalf just hours before by ECI's outside counsel, tried vainly to get bail set for his new client in Nassau County on the trespassing and stolen property charges. Rosen realized the Rockland and Bergen County prosecutors wanted her held interminably, but the veteran defense lawyer insisted on bond for Rita. He had sympathized with her plight immediately after fighting rush-hour traffic from Manhattan to get to the Second Precinct station house in Woodbury, which was engulfed with reporters, camera crews, and onlookers as he pulled in. Rosen had quickly met and consoled the frightened widow, while quickly grasping the case at hand. "This is a set-up!" Rosen told the reporters outside the precinct. Rosen insisted that Rita Gluzman had not done anything that would cause the woman to flee, that she certainly would show up in court to answer the burglary charges filed against her. Otherwise, there were no warrants outstanding anywhere for Rita Gluzman, Rosen said, and the trespassing complaint against Rita had been exaggerated because the authorities in Rockland couldn't pin any more serious crime on the confused woman, whose husband had been brutally murdered less than a week ago. She wasn't considered a suspect, and his client was disoriented, devastated by the events since then.

Judge Weinberg's no-bail decision would remain at least for the weekend, however, until a formal bail hearing was set for the following Tuesday in Mineola, when the senior state judge in Supreme Court there would entertain Rosen's motions for Gluzman's release. This was little consolation either to Rosen or to his new client, who was unaccustomed to sitting in a jailhouse, though Rita was no stranger to sacrifice, having starved herself outside the United Nations for more than two weeks when winning Yakov's freedom twenty-five years earlier. Still, it promised to be a lonely, wretched weekend for her, away from home already for a week, and, as it was discovered, an undetected guest at Cold Spring Harbor since Monday the 8th. A paralegal with Rosen loaned Gluzman her white linen jacket, as the handcuffed trespasser had been wearing only a lightweight spring outfit for two days, and the cool breeze of the early April evening was making her shiver.

Nassau was working in concert with Rockland, the two New York county DAs well aware of the implications of Rita's discovery at Cold Spring Harbor and her subsequent arrest and detention at Woodbury. Both Bongiorno and Denis Dillon, the Nassau prosecutor, respected the prerogative of the other to hold and return a suspect to the other's jurisdiction, though Rita was still formally not wanted for killing her husband. Rita

Gluzman might well have had nothing to do with Yakov's death, but until the missing woman had given a conclusive interview to authorities in New York State, it was important to them she not leave the U.S., even if her fears about an assassin of the Gluzman family had any foundation. At the same time, samples of the detectives' tests of fingerprints, blood, and hair from the Pearl River apartment were still being processed by the crime labs, to determine how much physical evidence there was of a second participant in the murder of Yakov Gluzman. Hoffmann, Colantonio, and Valvo were waiting for delivery from New Jersey of the evidence found in the two cars at One Madison Easter Sunday.

Disturbingly, the detectives noted, Rita Gluzman was not acting like a typical grieving widow. She seemed remorseless, it seemed to Colantonio and the others who saw her up close in Long Island, and her mysterious disappearance had only served to somehow validate Zelenin's statement that she had coerced him into the crime and abandoned him afterward. Nobody was sure how long she'd stay around if bail were issued.

But after Tuesday the 16th there was no certainty Rita could be detained in the Nassau jail, or anywhere, for much longer. Rosen had a card up his sleeve. The attorney announced that he planned a felony hearing, at Rita's Tuesday bail hearing, that would force the government's hand within the six-day period that had begun Friday to either charge his client in her husband's death, or show that the risk of her flight was so great as to limit bail. It was an educated gambit by Rosen: put up or shut up, he was telling the prosecutors. You got the evidence, charge her; otherwise, let her go. And Mike Rosen knew how slowly the law worked. If Rockland and Bergen didn't yet have sufficient proof of Rita's involvement in Yakov's murder and were still unsure by

Tuesday, the lawyer knew, the DAs were stretching, trying to buy time—and with his client's freedom, no less. Rosen had gotten clients released practically on their own recognizance when the government had far greater evidence against them of serious crimes, and he reassured Rita Gluzman he'd do everything he could on her behalf between Friday night and Tuesday morning.

But for now Rita Gluzman would spend the weekend in the Nassau County jail, while her attorney prepared for the week ahead.

Simply because all factors pointed toward Rita Gluzman as a contributing player in Yakov Gluzman's murder wasn't sufficient evidence for the DA to win an indictment of her at the state level or even to continue holding her. The law provided that protection, and substantiated facts were required, not just the accusation of an admitted murderer, the suspicions of prosecutors in three different counties in two states, or the conventional wisdom of the reporters covering the sordid week-long affair. The evidence didn't assemble itself overnight. Laboratory blood tests can take weeks in many instances, especially when their results are of crucial forensic importance to a serious criminal investigation. Rita's disappearance, whether or not it had been generally thought of as "flight" by anyone vaguely following the case, had to be proven to be cause for the court to think she might attempt to leave the state, or the country. After all, there had been no warrants outstanding for Gluzman's arrest when she had left New Jersey the previous Sunday, or any that she was aware of during the five days she was missing, and even with the extenuating circumstances of her husband's coldblooded killing, she was entitled to the benefit of the doubt. Rita's police record was clean, except for a shoplifting incident the previous January. As far as her trespassing charge at Cold Spring Harbor Labs was concerned, the only actual damage done by Rita had been when she'd broken a screen door while avoiding the security director. She could easily reimburse CSHL the $20 for the screen door, and the trespass charge would have been no greater than a misdemeanor. Possession of the stolen license plates was a slightly more serious charge, but combined with the Cold Spring Harbor complaint would have resulted only in a simple bail release for most first offenders in Nassau or any other New York county, with no extenuating circumstances.

Further, Rosen had argued, every asset Rita Gluzman owned was within an hour of the Nassau County courthouse: ECI, the Upper Saddle River home. Rita wasn't cash-rich; if she were going to leave the country, she'd have to liquidate stocks, certificates of deposit, and the authorities would know to stop her, right? So why keep Rita in jail? What had she done to merit this incarceration before a trial?

Tuesday, April 16, at the felony hearing in Mineola, Rosen's motion and arguments appeared meritorious and successful until the senior judge, Thomas W. Dwyer, denied the lawyer's request to lower the charges against Rita and provide for bail. Still, without a felony charge against her in the next 48 hours, she would be released. The Rockland prosecutors had to act quickly if they wanted to keep Rita within arms' reach, as Valvo and Bongiorno feared she would indeed use one of her two passports and other resources to leave the U.S. Rita traveled extensively on business to Israel, which, like Switzerland, refused to extradite criminal suspects to

the United States. The DAs suspected she wasn't anxious
to stay for a trial.

Now the clock was ticking furiously in Mike Bongiorno's office, and on the other side of the corridor
in Lou Valvo's command room. Less than two days
remained before Rita's automatic release in Nassau
County, and if she were to be charged with the more
serious crime Rockland needed to act. Once more Bongiorno called across the Hudson to Deirdre Daly and
Cathy Seibel in the U.S. Attorney's office.

Seibel told Daly and Bongiorno that a colleague,
Marjorie Miller, had pointed out to her a recently
enacted provision of the 1994 Federal Crime Bill, known
as the Violence Against Women Act, a part of the major
legislation which had among other things provided for
midnight basketball and more police on the streets; it
had been an "omnibus" bill in all its scope. Miller
revealed to Seibel and Daly that it was now a specific
felony for someone to cross state lines in order to abuse
or, worse, kill a spouse. Federal guidelines provided for
serious sentences, including life without parole. Perhaps
Rita Gluzman might qualify for prosecution under this
law, Seibel told them, if the DA thought she'd been
involved in Yakov Gluzman's murder. Though state
prosecution was the normal way to deal with a murder
case, time was of the essence if Rockland felt Rita should
be held, and the crime scene evidence from East Rutherford was still in transit.

Something among the items in Zelenin's Taurus and
Gluzman's Maxima might help them with their conclu-
sions, whether the ax, hatchet, gloves, or possibly the
Henckel knives found.

Into Wednesday the conversations between Rockland

and White Plains continued, with the DA and the U.S. attorneys reviewing the Violence Against Women Act, what they knew about the crime in their backyard, and what they had come to believe about Rita Gluzman and her possible involvement. Bongiorno, Valvo, Daly, and Seibel came to a conclusion: Rita Gluzman was about to make history. She would be the first woman to be charged under the Violence Against Women Act, which had made it a federal criminal offense to cross state lines in order to abuse and kill a spouse. A law whose sponsors envisioned battered women in need of protection from violent husbands could also provide justice and solace for the survivors of a man abused and killed, reportedly, by his wife. And the budget of the federal prosecutors was big enough to pursue justice while not crippling taxpayers. All they would have to do would be to arrest Rita Gluzman.

Eight

Around the U.S. on Thursday, April 18, several justice stories were playing out. In Los Angeles, the Menendez brothers had been sentenced to life in prison for killing their parents, convicted at last after seven years and two trials and sent away for an infamous, gruesome crime that had consumed public awareness since 1989, when the two had killed their father and mother. In Florida, F. Lee Bailey, the renowned criminal defense attorney whose most recent "last hurrah" had been during the O.J. Simpson murder trial, was about to be released from a federal prison where he had spent six months for failing to turn over to the government a large sum he'd appropriated from a criminal client.

In New York, reporters covering a murder case were waiting to learn the fate of Rita Gluzman, a forty-seven-year-old woman whose husband had been butchered into little pieces twelve days before. In that time, Rita had become the most obvious suspect in her husband's death, and stories in the daily newspapers reminded readers that while she wasn't officially wanted for murder it was only a matter of time before the law would catch up with the Ukrainian-born businesswoman. Her cousin had admitted disposing of Yakov's body and had insisted that Rita had taken part in the killing. And now Vladimir Zelenin was being transported in a Rockland County Sheriff's car to New City, New York, from Hackensack, New Jersey, to testify against the cousin he claimed had betrayed him and her husband.

Michael Bongiorno and Lou Valvo finally knew the whereabouts of the missing link in their open murder case, the victim's wife, which was no empty victory to the prosecutors even with one participant's earlier admission of guilt.

The DAs and the detectives had looked at the motives both Vladimir Zelenin and Rita Gluzman might have had, searching for an explanation as to why either would have killed an innocent man in such a gruesome manner. If the confessed killer was telling the truth, both of them had carved up the microbiologist to prevent him from leaving his wife. The investigators had ruled out romantic gain as a motive for either of them. While Zelenin had abundant economic desperation, it did not appear that his impoverished existence had led him to commit a murder for hire. There was no evidence of any money flowing to him, and his confession had eliminated the possibility of any personal financial gain for the illegal immigrant, as it would be nearly a lifetime before he could enjoy it. The detectives could find only one money link between Zelenin and Yakov, letters in the two men's apartments that confirmed the loan Yakov had made to Vladimir to settle the dilemma that the handyman had with his cousin Gregory Kogan in Brooklyn.

Rita's motive seemed very clear to the investigators, and the DA was looking for a legally safe way to indict her. Zelenin's motive was also clear: the handyman was under siege from all sides, and had acted to protect his meager existence and to avoid being deported to Kyrgyzstan, a truly abysmal place that inspired in him only fear, increasing his desperation to the point where it had pushed him over the edge. Organized crime had nothing to gain from the killing of a prestigious scientist like Yakov Gluzman, and the cancer researcher had no apparent connection to the violent racketeers in the Russian mob who had settled in Brooklyn since the end of the Soviet Union.

Valvo's indictment of Zelenin which the county grand jury had handed up had satisfied the DA that with the man's confession in hand there would be little problem guaranteeing lifetime incarceration to Rita's cousin. Now that he was in their custody, the DA and Colantonio visited their new prisoner in the jail two blocks away in the government office complex. Valvo told the Russian that he appreciated the statement the killer had made in New Jersey and his offer to cooperate with the authorities in New York. But the DA reminded the Russian of his need to understand two things: first, the man's confession was enough to send him to prison for the rest of his life, as Zelenin's blood and fingerprints were all over Yakov Gluzman's apartment. Second, perhaps more important to Zelenin, neither Valvo nor the government needed him or his testimony at all to find possible accomplices and prosecute them.

In the event the man's story checked out, and his cousin Rita Gluzman had been a participant in her husband's murder, Zelenin's cooperation as a witness would be noted by the prosecutor and he would inform the court of the man's help. But the DA would not offer any substantial reduction in sentence to him in exchange for his testimony. Did he still wish to talk about the crime?

Yes, Zelenin told him. He suggested to Valvo and Colantonio through the new Russian interpreter that he realized his life was over. He understood the rules of engagement, and said he was thankful that Richard Freeman hadn't executed him at the Madison parking lot after discovering his crime. The authorities in Kyrgyzstan would not have thought twice about shooting him in the head. There was only one thing he was concerned for: his two young sons, who lived in Fair Lawn, New Jersey, in the apartment owned by ECI that Rita had provided while he worked there. Zelenin's wife had been killed two years earlier, in Russia, and he'd escaped with his sons to the U.S., where he tried to provide some semblance of security for them. As long as he knew his teenage sons wouldn't be deported and orphaned overseas, he was willing to cooperate with the DA and anybody else who wanted to know the details of the murder. Zelenin told them he knew he'd probably never see the outside world again.

But there was more, Zelenin told them. He'd kept recordings of phone conversations he and Rita had had in March, when they had planned the crime. Zelenin had decided he couldn't trust his cousin, so he had made a point of recording talks he had with Rita and had kept the tapes safely hidden at his apartment. She had fled, hadn't she? He was angry that Rita had run away and left him to take the fall entirely for the brutal murder of her husband, a crime that was her idea and from which she would benefit exclusively. What was worse, the prisoner continued, Yakov Gluzman had been maybe the only person in America who had been nice to him. Yakov had loaned him money to settle an immigration problem, and had asked nothing in return. This gnawed at the prisoner. He'd been fool enough to go along with Rita's plan to kill her husband, Zelenin said. I deserve to die, simply for being so weak, the prisoner told them.

Again, Valvo reminded him, you realize that you need us more than we need you, yes? Even if you eventually cooperate in a case against Rita Gluzman. That is, assuming she's ever found and assuming, more importantly, that we ever decide to charge her with anything. And you realize that, even if Rita is alive, and even if we ever decide there might be a case against her, that we can't guarantee you anything other than a trial, even if your statement helps us?

Zelenin assured the two men that he was ready for his great reward, so long as he knew his sons would survive in the U.S. But he would never be able to live with himself for having helped Rita kill Yakov Gluzman.

Valvo and Colantonio thought they had heard a pretty convincing story. Colantonio had had suspicions about Zelenin's confession at East Rutherford Sunday night, but the detective's doubts of its completeness began to ease as the week went on.

Then the FBI had provided them with a bombshell. When the New Jersey State Police had issued its "nationwide alert" for Rita the night of Zelenin's capture, a routine query had gone out to Interpol from the bureau's Washington office, informing the international police organization it was believed the missing woman, who enjoyed dual citizenship, might be headed for Israel, where she traveled for business. When it was learned on Tuesday the 9th that the body parts found in East Rutherford were indeed Yakov Gluzman's, that

news had made its way around the world, and was
reported widely in the Israeli press, both in Hebrew and
English. During the five-day search for Rita, the FBI
had checked occasionally with its overseas law contacts,
searching for word of Rita's whereabouts.

Interpol in Jerusalem sent the FBI a report that con-
tained disturbing news: a private investigator in Tel Aviv
had come forward after hearing the news of Yakov Gluzman's death to tell them he had been hired by Rita
Gluzman seven months earlier, in September 1995, to
follow Yakov Gluzman while he visited his family in
Hadera. The investigator, David Rom, had done this,
he told the Hadera police, as it seemed like the usual
matrimonial situation, where a husband or wife suspected the other of cheating on them. Only this had
turned out to be quite different than the usual matrimonial tail. The investigator had taken photos of Yakov
with Raisa Korenblit when the scientist had been out
with the Israeli woman. That was standard operating
procedure, he explained. The woman paid him for the
photos and he thought nothing more of the job until
he identified one of the pictures of Yakov and Raisa
he'd sent his client in New Jersey in the evidence book
at the Hadera police station. The photo had been used
in an extortion case reported to the police in December.
Someone had written Michael and Chaim Gluzman, the
scientist's brother and father, threatening to expose
Yakov's "philandering," as the letterwriter phrased it,
unless the Gluzman family paid a large sum to the extortionist, who remained anonymous.

Rom had just learned of the existence of the photos,
along with the death of Yakov Gluzman, and had
become suspicious of Rita almost immediately, so he
reported his involvement with the ECI widow to the
Hadera authorities. The Interpol report said the private

investigator had suspicions that she'd been involved in Yakov's murder.

Making its way through law enforcement channels, the Interpol release had reached Rockland early in the investigation's second week. The FBI agent assigned to the case had found and forwarded it to the Rockland detectives.

Now, the DA reasoned, if this report were true, they had just learned that Rita tried to blackmail her husband's family in the months before he was murdered, hiring private investigators overseas to tail Yakov, who had separated from her en route to a divorce. Why?

The case centered entirely on Yakov and Rita, the DA concluded. Other than Rita Gluzman, only cancer cells stood to gain anything from the biologist's death.

The reporters covering the murder case had learned what the detectives had found in their investigation into Rita Gluzman. Like Yakov, she was born in the Ukraine after World War II, growing up toward the height of the Cold War behind the Iron Curtain, where mobility of Ukrainian citizens, especially Jews, was limited due to the attitudes of the ethnic Russians who had closed the border to the west after the war. Kiev, Odessa, and other cities in the Ukraine had been the most devastated by the war. Poland lay to the west, and Romania to the south, leaving the Ukraine, one of the original Soviet Republics, to form the Communist country after the 1917 revolution, isolated from the western democracies. Economically distraught following World War II, young people and their families there who had survived the destruction of the war scrambled in any way possible to make ends meet. Rita had been born on July 27, 1948, a year after Yakov. While the Ukraine would boast one of the largest Jewish populations in the world, Jews were still a minority there, three or four percent of the population. Moreover, it had been politically acceptable after 1945 in the Ukraine, as in other eastern European countries, to blame the surviving Jews for the brutal war that had just claimed untold millions of lives, and genuine anti-Semitism was rampant throughout Poland, Belarus, and the Ukraine. This postwar upbringing had formed a survivalist mindset in both Rita Shapiro and Yasha Gluzman, who met while teenagers.

Rita married Yakov Gluzman just as he graduated from Moscow State University with a degree in biology in 1969. The newlyweds had begun plans to emigrate to Israel. At the height of the Cold War during the 1960s it was not an advantage to be Jewish in the Soviet Union, if one had ambitions beyond permanent servitude to the state. Traditional orthodox Christianity was at least tolerated, but the Soviet state was unofficially anti-Semitic in its policies, and no prominent leaders of either the Communist party, its Secretariat, the Politburu that ran the state, or the Russian military were Jewish. It was, in short, not reassuring to be Jewish in the Soviet Union.

Yakov Gluzman and his new wife Rita couldn't wait to leave for Israel, where the promising scientist could achieve much more than in Moscow. Rita's exit visa was approved. Yakov's was not. The government had had plans for him, based on what they had learned from his instructors at Moscow State. While Yasha Gluzman wasn't an ethnic Russian, he could at least aid the Communist defense effort, whether he wanted to or not. They would not let him become another statistic in the Brain Drain that had seen so many of the brighter scientists defect to the west. This was the beginning of the newlyweds' first crisis. Yakov dropped out of Moscow

State to train as a carpenter, thinking the government would no longer try to restrain his exit if he weren't a promising scientist. But the plan didn't work; they hadn't fooled the bureaucrats with his carpentry ruse.

In early 1970, Yasha and Rita made a pact. Rita would exercise her privilege to patriate to Israel with her family, the members of which had also been granted visas, while Yakov remained in Moscow for a while. Rita would do everything within her power to free her new husband, whatever it would take. The couple would eventually be reunited in the Jewish homeland and restart their lives together. Somehow, Rita promised, she would get her husband freed from the ruthlessness of the Soviet state.

Rita arrived in Tel Aviv in the spring of 1970 full of hope, and the Shapiros settled. She quickly learned that winning freedom for Yakov would not be simple, and that numerous obstacles lay ahead. But her determination would be proved over the course of the next two years. Rita learned shortly after landing in Israel that she was pregnant, and Yakov would be a father before the end of 1970, though he wouldn't be present at his son's birth. Ilan Gluzman was born in December 1970 in Tel Aviv, and Rita had gotten word to Yakov both of his new son and of her persistence in trying to get him out of Moscow and reunited with the family in Israel.

Pressing every legal channel she knew in Israel, Rita had tried to make Yakov Gluzman's emigration from Moscow a paramount item in the lives of the officials in Tel Aviv, but they had been unsuccessful in convincing the Soviet embassy that Yakov should be allowed to leave the confines of Moscow's military and science establishment. His professors at Moscow State had given him too many glowing reviews. In 1971 Rita made a bold move: she approached the United Nations and the U.S. Congress, finding a sympathetic ear in Benjamin

Rosenthal, a fourth-term New York City Representative
with a strong track record in supporting both Jewish
causes and the fledgling movement in the U.S. that
worked on behalf of Soviet Jewry. Rosenthal was a member of the important House Foreign Affairs Committee
and chairman of its subcommittee on Europe, which
conducted hearings on the problems of Soviet Jews in
November 1971.

It had been nearly two years since Rita had seen Yasha,
but her hard work was paying off: the American Jewish
Committee was now well aware of Yakov's plight, and
Rosenthal was pressing the Nixon adminstration and
Secretary of State William Rogers, as well as Soviet
Ambassador Anatoly Dobrynin, to grant Yakov permis-
sion to leave Moscow and be with his family.

But even that high-level diplomatic initiative didn't
work. Although the AJC petitioned both Dobrynin and
the President of the UN General Assembly, Adam Malik,
on behalf of more than a thousand Soviet Jews wishing
to leave Russia, regular channels were time-consuming.
And the Nixon administration was acting cautiously with
Moscow. The war in Vietnam was the most important
issue both to a majority of Americans as well as to the
administration, and American leaders, particularly
Nixon and his national security advisor, Henry Kis-
singer, himself a liberated German Jew, wanted freedom
for Soviet Jews but needed to maintain diplomatic equil-
brium with Moscow. While it might be a useful bar-
gaining chip in trying to stalemate the Cold War, the
plight of scientists such as Yakov Gluzman wouldn't be
allowed to interfere with more serious matters, such as
the possibility of a nuclear war between the reigning
superpowers.

Rita showed great strength and perseverance in playing her next card: she protested directly in front of the

UN, then went on a hunger strike, seeking attention for Yakov's plight. She drew enormous attention along First Avenue during her eighteen-day fast, and finally embarrassed officials of the Russian embassy cabled Moscow suggesting there was more to gain from granting an exit visa to Yakov Gluzman than by keeping the scientist in Moscow against his will while the world watched his wife starve in front of the television cameras. The Soviets folded. Rita Gluzman had won her first major victory.

With his exit visa approved, in December 1971 Yasha arrived in Tel Aviv to meet his year-old son and embrace his courageous wife for the first time in almost two years. Yasha then enrolled at the prestigious Weizmann Institute, which is to Israel what MIT or Cal Tech are to the U.S. Rita, too, enrolled at Weizmann, where she studied chemistry while Yakov did doctoral work in microbiology. The couple left for the U.S. in 1977, after Yasha was hired by Cold Spring Harbor Labs to begin his career as a cancer researcher. Yakov won fame for his study, then was recruited by Lederle to head up its biology division. Rita raised Ilan, then started ECI, fulfilling her business ambitions after raising her son. The couple had apparently realized the American dream of material success and great mobility.

Bongiorno, Valvo, and Colantonio wondered, was this the face of evil, or a simple crime of passion gone awry? The flow of evidence suggesting Rita Gluzman had helped kill her husband was becoming larger each day, and the Interpol report had cinched the DA's resolve to charge her for the crime, whichever way was most effective. The DA then made a crucial decision. He would turn the case over to Deirdre Daly and Cathy Seibel for federal prosecution. They had enough to make a case. But the prosecutors had to act quickly.

Nine

Judge Dwyer changed his mind and established bail in Nassau County late Thursday morning, setting Rita Gluzman's bond at $250,000. It was a rather large amount for five days of squatting, a broken screen door, and stealing a set of license plates, but Rita was likely to win release on the trespassing charges anyway, and she couldn't be held interminably, even if she had become a suspect in Yakov Gluzman's killing, without a criminal warrant and extradition request. It made little sense to the prosecutor or the judge to let her walk out the door of their jail without some financial sacrifice. Rita's attorney and accountant at ECI guaranteed the bond with the Upper Saddle River home. If Rita were, as the detectives feared, going to flee overseas, it would cost her.

Lou Valvo and Steve Colantonio were notified of the court's decision, and vigorously plied their cell phones to both Nassau and White Plains in a rush to seize

Gluzman before she submitted the bond and walked out of the Nassau jail. Seibel already had prepared a federal complaint charging Rita with crossing state lines to abuse a spouse resulting in death, the first time the new law would be used against a woman. But first they had to get to Long Island and arrest her.

Shortly after 4 P.M. while Mike Rosen was driving back to Manhattan from Mineola, where he'd arranged for Rita's bail, his car phone rang. It was George Gabriel, a veteran FBI agent who'd nailed mob boss John Gotti six years earlier and remembered Rosen favorably as the lawyer for Gotti's co-defendant, Thomas Gambino. Gotti had been convicted while Gambino was acquitted, but Gabriel had borne no hard feelings toward the astute Rosen. As a professional courtesy, the FBI agent had called to tell Rosen that his new client was about to be arrested, this time on federal charges, and that he might want to return to Mineola. Rosen thanked the lawman, hung up, cursed, and got off the Grand Central Expressway to turn around and race back to the Nassau courthouse. The lawyer arrived in time to see Rita leaving the clerk's station, having been released after the bond had been accepted. The next thing the lawyer saw was two FBI agents approach, then arrest, his client. Gluzman was feeling faint, but Rosen helped her to remain on her feet. The attorney reassured his client that it would be only a matter of time before her arraignment and bail hearing in federal court. First, she had to be processed, and the FBI took her to the Westchester County jail in Valhalla, twenty-five miles north of Manhattan, where she'd be booked as a federal prisoner.

Lou Valvo breathed a sigh of relief and called Mike Bongiorno in New City to tell the DA the good news. The two prosecutors laughed as they joked about the loss of Court TV and CNN discovering the Rockland courthouse, but reminded one another that their work was just beginning. In less than a week they'd been able to organize an airtight case, it seemed, against the person they believed had been Vladimir Zelenin's accomplice, and cause an arrest. Zelenin's guilty plea had been entered into Rockland court earlier in the day, and his statement read into the New York State jurisdiction's record.

If Bongiorno and Valvo had charged Rita Gluzman at the state level, the law provided for no better than a second-degree murder prosecution, and if Rita were convicted in New York state court in Rockland, her maximum sentence would be fifteen years. She most likely would walk out of prison in half that time. Bongiorno had sacrificed whatever prosecutorial glory he might have gotten by handing the case to the U.S. Attorney, whom he liked and felt was capable of convicting Rita Gluzman on the interstate abuse charge. If she were found guilty in federal court, Rita faced life without parole, which in the federal system meant just that. It was decided Valvo would join Daly and Seibel as liaison from the DA in preparing for trial.

There was little dispute at this point among any of the prosecutors as to Rita's culpability. It certainly seemed she'd contributed to her husband's death. But it was still perplexing to all why Yasha Gluzman had been killed the way he had. Why had the killers—and forensics suggested two killers at this point—so gruesomely dismembered the scientist as though he were a lab experiment? A simple bullet would have sufficed, as would any number of other methods gentler than axes and hatchets. Whose idea was the Henckel knives?

* * *

Mike Rosen made every argument he knew to get bail for Rita at the Westchester County jail, where she was held as a federal prisoner indefinitely. Initially, Deirdre Daly and Cathy Seibel argued in their complaint that no bail should be granted until Rita's trial, which would be scheduled to begin six months after her processing. Rosen filed a motion requesting bail for Rita, maintaining as he had in Nassau County that she presented neither danger nor flight, but the lawyer knew he'd have to petition for a hearing before the senior magistrate in White Plains Federal Court in order to get bail for Rita before trial. The government was simply unwilling to agree to any bail for Rita Gluzman.

Rosen called an associate, Diarmuid White, an expert in pre-trial motions who'd been successful in winning bail for some of Rosen's other criminal clients. White worked for a week on Gluzman's bail motion, collecting cases, sorting them out in the war room of Rosen's suite of offices in lower Wall Street. Along with Mike Davis, Rosen's associate, the attorneys began to study the laws that were cited in Rita's arrest. Now that their client was held under a federal warrant, any arguments and prior decisions the attorneys used would have to be based on federal cases.

In the criminal cause for detention hearing in White Plains on April 26, Rosen, Mike Davis, and Diarmuid White appeared on Rita Gluzman's behalf to plead for her release before trial on the federal charges. Cathy Seibel argued the U.S. Attorney's case against any bail for the accused, repeating their fear of her flight. Rita's disappearance for five days was a major issue.

Seibel opened. "Your Honor, the government has moved for detention on the grounds of flight risk and dangerousness. On the flight risk, Your Honor, there is overwhelming proof that this defendant is likely to flee if released. Perhaps the most obvious proof is that she has already fled once in this case."

Then, reviewing the facts of the period between the discovery of Zelenin's disposal of Yakov's body parts Easter Sunday through the discovery of Gluzman a week later at Cold Spring Harbor, Seibel revealed what the detectives had learned since that Friday two weeks before: the telephone records from the room Rita had hidden in at Cold Spring Harbor showed calls to seven airline companies, all of them carriers with overseas destinations on direct flights out of Kennedy airport, twenty minutes from Cold Spring Harbor. The phone company had been able to trace every call made from the cabin, to the toll-free numbers of the airline companies. And, Seibel continued, Gluzman had called neighbors in Upper Saddle River during the week, asking if they would get her secondary passport out of the Gluzman house. She had torn a business card into shreds which the police lab had reconstructed, and it bore the name of a private banker at the Union Bank of Switzerland.

Seibel gave the defense team a preview of what the government might show at the trial. She told Magistrate Mark Fox that as far as "dangerousness" was concerned, "the nature of the offense speaks for itself. This was a planned execution and butchering. It is as gruesome and violent a crime as you will see." Seibel stated the various detectives' findings, such as a tape recorder Rita had placed behind Yakov's refrigerator at Pearl River, and the strains of the couple's divorce proceedings, then summarized her point for Fox.

"Your Honor, if this defendant is willing to go to these lengths to gain an advantage on her husband in divorce litigation, it doesn't require much of a stretch of the imagination to believe attempts would be made at obstruction in this case were she to be released on bail." Downplaying the value of the financial package offered by Rita Gluzman to assure her honoring bail, Seibel pointed out that the family house Rosen and Gluzman had committed was negligible, having been mortgaged almost to its equity, and that by Rita's own admission, ECI was barely profitable. While Rita had access to assets and some cash, that which she'd pledged toward bail while she awaited a serious trial some six months in the future was not of significant enough value to keep anyone around. It was clear Rita Gluzman had little motivation to remain in the U.S. if she was let out of jail now.

Rosen tried to explain that Gluzman was an internationally-known businesswoman, and that the travel books found with her were readily available in any bookstore, and hadn't represented any specific "hiding place" for his client. Rita's defense attorney also explained that her sister and mother lived near her in New Jersey, but the rest of his argument for Gluzman's release on bail was challenging as he tried to put Rita in a favorable light. She had run out on her family, it seemed; and little about New Jersey seemed enough to keep her in the Garden State during the time after Yakov's death. Rosen tried to show that ECI's employees were depending on her to run the company, though she'd walked out on them, too, during the week she was away. He also spoke positively about Rita Gluzman's scientific background. Rosen tried to introduce Rita's being granted bail in Nassau County, after her six-day incarceration, as evidence of that jurisdiction's granting her freedom even when she was thought to be a murder suspect in another county. But the bail had been

$250,000 on a charge that amounted to "theft of services," a steep amount for such a charge. Rosen introduced other bail cases in his long experience where the defendant had been able to post bond using an entire asset portfolio. He spent nearly an hour pleading with Fox to grant Rita Gluzman some freedom as she awaited trial.

But it was to no avail. The magistrate judge decided that Gluzman's abandonment of both her family and ECI during the six day period following her husband's death led his court to determine that the widow was indeed a "flight risk" and that it would be unlikely Rita Gluzman would stay around for her trial. But he gave the attorneys another week to present both stronger arguments and a better financial package of the assets of the accused that would somehow reassure the government of her better intentions. That, Fox told Rosen and White, they could provide at Rita's pre-trial hearing in a week or two.

For now, Rita Gluzman would spend at least another week locked up at the Westchester County jail in Valhalla, ten minutes north of White Plains. There was a small holding facility at the jail for women, and another for federal prisoners. During that time, prosecutors Cathy Seibel and Marjorie Groban would prepare an indictment that they would present to a federal grand jury the following week. Rita had been arrested and preliminarily charged in connection with her husband's death, but formal charges against her needed the approval of the grand jury. As this was now a federal prosecution, Daly and Seibel would have to prove that the crime had occurred within their jurisdiction, the Southern District of New York, and that any charges against Rita Gluzman for any crimes would have to show a presence in the six-county area that comprised that district.

As the murder of Yakov Gluzman had occurred in Pearl River, a hamlet in Rockland County that was part of Daly's district, there would be little problem on that issue; Rita Gluzman had traveled north from the Gluzman home in Upper Saddle River, New Jersey, to purportedly kill her husband Yakov with her cousin Vladimir Zelenin, so the crossing-of-state-lines statute was fulfilled to justify the use of the Crime Bill's Violence Against Women act. And Rita, when fleeing New Jersey Easter Sunday, had traveled across the George Washington Bridge, connecting Bergen County with upper Manhattan across the Hudson River. Manhattan was another of the six counties in the Southern District, and Gluzman had driven through Manhattan and through the borough of Queens to arrive at Cold Spring Harbor on Long Island. Although Queens and Long Island were in New York's Eastern District, the fact that Rita traveled through Daly's jurisdiction would be satisfactory, together with the Pearl River crime scene, to prove venue. The details were quite different from state court, and the prosecutors would have to be thorough in their proof of Gluzman's whereabouts in order to satisfy the law.

Mike Rosen and Diarmuld White, joined by Mike Davis, were examining the 1994 Crime Bill and its novel provisions, one of which was being used to incarcerate their client, whom the government had no desire to see set free while she awaited trial.

Vladimir Zelenin had started talking to Lou Valvo and Steve Colantonio, joined at times by Tom Hoffmann, and was telling the Rockland investigators every detail the Russian could recall about the crime and his

relationship with Rita Gluzman. Rita and he had left
Yasha's Pearl River apartment twice the night of the
killing: first, after striking the death blow before midnight, to go to the house in Upper Saddle River to wash
off, then return to Pearl River to begin the task of
dissecting Yakov's body in the tiny bathtub in his one-
bedroom apartment. Then around eight o'clock Sunday
morning, which was actually only seven by their body
clocks, owing to the changeover to Daylight Savings
Time, he and Rita had, Zelenin told them, left again
for New Jersey, this time with Yakov's body parts stowed
in the trunks of two cars, Zelenin's Taurus and Yasha's
Maxima, which Rita had driven. Along the way, they
had stopped in Fair Lawn, Zelenin's town in New Jersey,
where Rita bought bandages to wrap wounds on Zelenin's hand. He told the cops, the wounds were the result
of a wild swing Rita had taken in the dark of Yakov's
apartment when they had attacked the scientist as he
entered his front door. Rita had cut into her accomplice's hand instead.

In checking out Zelenin's story in the nearly three-
week period since his arrest, FBI Special Agent Hilda
Kogut and Joseph Higgins had interviewed the clerk at
the CVS drugstore in Paramus, New Jersey, where Zelenin said he and Rita had stopped early Sunday morning
to get bandages. After reviewing the records of Easter
Sunday, the store manager found the clerk, Lenny Huffman, who had been working that morning, and when
Kogut talked with the man, he identified Rita Gluzman
from a picture she showed him. Huffman remembered
his customer. At first, he had thought she'd bought a
lot of bandages for one person and had asked if she
was okay. All was well, the customer had told the drugstore clerk. Later, Huffman said he'd seen Rita's picture

on the news, but hadn't linked the purchase with Gluzman's escape. He hadn't seen Vladimir Zelenin.

Of itself, the drugstore clerk's recollection wasn't
enough. But when the investigators checked the bandages and receipt found in Zelenin's Taurus at One
Madison against the records from the CVS cash register,
they were a match.

Valvo and Seibel had looked at the interview records
concerning the bandage purchase. It would have been
a "cosmic coincidence," in Deirdre Daly's words, for
Rita Gluzman to have visited a drugstore early Sunday
morning four towns away in New Jersey, bought a large
quantity of bandages, then somehow misplaced those
bandages so that they ended up in the car of Vladimir
Zelenin and, in fact, on Zelenin's right hand, exactly
at the time when her cousin had needed one to close
a wound received when he had been killing Rita's husband. The CVS interview added corroborative evidence
to the prosecution's case against Rita Gluzman.

Israel checked in again, in the form of a newspaper
story in the respected daily *Yehidiot Ahronot,* detailing the
police investigation in Hadera, where Yakov Gluzman's
father, mother, and brother lived, into the extortion
plot against the Gluzman family that had occurred the
previous fall. The two Israeli private detectives who'd
spoken to the Hadera police the week before were now
recalling Rita Gluzman as a woman obsessed with ending her husband's liaison with Raisa Korenblit. Why
would Rita, who contested the divorce action, want pictures of Yasha and Raisa? Since she and Yakov were
separated, Rita couldn't sue her husband for adultery
in New Jersey. And how had one of the pictures taken
by the investigators for their American client, shipped
to her at her New Jersey office by Federal Express, end
up as evidence in an open extortion case in Hadera?

It took no great leap of imagination on the part of Lou Valvo or Cathy Seibel to conclude that Rita Gluzman could have tried to extort an amount they later learned to be $100,000 from Chaim Gluzman, Yakov's father, by threatening the older Gluzman with the exposure of Yakov's assignations with the younger Korenblit to the Israeli press if the anonymous extortionist weren't paid. In the extortionist's second letter, he or she had demanded an additional $50,000. The letters had both been mailed from Tel Aviv, using Israeli postage, in October and early December of 1995. Rita Gluzman had traveled on business to Israel in September.

Thursday, May 8, came, and Rita was placed in the Valhalla jail's high-security van for the ride south to the White Plains federal courthouse on Quarropas Street, where the widow of Yakov Gluzman was ushered to a quiet courtroom upstairs. Deirdre Daly and Cathy Seibel were waiting for her, along with Lou Valvo, who had been designated a Special Assistant U.S. Attorney by Daly and her boss Mary Jo White for the duration of the case. During Gluzman's formal arraignment on charges of "crossing state lines to abuse a spouse resulting in death," Deirdre Daly read the indictment on the joint federal and state charges before U.S. Magistrate Judge Lisa Margaret Smith, who scheduled the preliminary hearing for the following Monday in the White Plains courthouse and assigned Judge Barrington Parker, Jr., to the case. Due to the seriousness of the charges, the bail issue was now moot. Rita Gluzman would have to get used to close quarters for the time being, or at least until her attorneys could acquit her at the trial. Technically, under federal law the government had seventy days to proceed with a trial after an arraignment, though Cathy Seibel wouldn't commit to a firm start date. And in the federal arena, it was possible to waive the seventy-day requirement. New York State law requires the local DA to try a case within six months of arrest or indictment or see the case dismissed. The term "speedy trial" has varying meanings. The marshals took Rita back to Valhalla.

Ten

The investigators were working overtime analyzing all the articles of evidence they had collected in the murder case. They now had both a confessed participant in the crime, who claimed to have landed the death blow and was caught with the victim's body, and they had an indicted suspect thought to be his accomplice, against whom the confessed party, now a government witness, would testify. Both were in custody.

Working full-time in the case known as U.S. v. Rita Gluzman were the Rockland County detectives led by Tom Hoffmann and Steve Colantonio, the Rockland County Sheriff's Office, in the person of Jake Szpicek, the DA, represented by Lou Valvo, and Special Agent Hilda Kogut of the FBI, an eighteen-year veteran who worked out of the Bureau's Newburgh office north of Rockland. Cathy Seibel was in charge of the U.S. Attorney's prosecution, and she and Valvo pored over numerous documents and lab tests from the search of the

Pearl River apartment, the Taurus and Maxima found in East Rutherford, Interpol reports on the extortion plot in Israel, and interviews with anyone who might prove a valuable witness.

After interviewing Vladimir Zelenin over a month-long period, the entire prosecution team was convinced his statement was true, and nobody harbored any doubts about Rita Gluzman's complicity in killing her husband. The U.S. Attorney added federal conspiracy charges to Gluzman's indictment, due to her planning Yakov's execution with her cousin. Zelenin would stay in the Rockland jail at least until Rita's trial, when he would testify that she had intimidated him into killing Yakov. The prisoner hoped he might see the outside world again before he died. He had been reassured of his sons' safety when his parents had come from Kyrgyzstan to care for the boys, and Valvo had promised none of them would be deported as long as he kept his promise to testify against Rita.

Even if his testimony were used successfully against Rita Gluzman at her trial, Zelenin realized the rosiest reward for his efforts would be a reduction in time from life to at best twenty years. Nearing forty, Zelenin realized that many years away in a maximum security prison, where, because of the nature of his crime, there would be no additional benefits granted for good behavior, amounted to a life sentence.

Zelenin's fingerprints were everywhere, on the body, on the tools used to kill Yakov Gluzman, inside Yakov's apartment. He'd been found with the dismembered remains of the victim, dumping the scientist into the Passaic. His hand was bloodied, cut badly, the result of a wound from one of the murder weapons found in the Taurus. Those facts alone supported his claim to have taken part in the killing of his cousin's husband. Zelenin's confession at East Rutherford, made after he had been read his Miranda rights, was enough to charge and convict him of murder, however his guilty plea in Rockland Court had made that point moot.

The Russian mafia had established a threatening presence in New York during the mid 1980s. Tales of the brutality of its members chilled law enforcement personnel assigned to investigate murders, extortion, price-rigging, and other felonies criminals from the former Soviet Union had committed in an area once known mainly for its *La Cosa Nostra* criminals. Dismemberment of victims was a common practice among strong-arm soldiers of the Russian mob, as opposed to the traditional shooting prevalent among American gangsters. While the Westies, New York's legendary Irish mob, had chopped their victims into pieces at times, it was rare as a method for executing rivals, enemies, and others. The Russians, though, seemed to think nothing of carving up those they dealt with, disposing of fingerprints, throwing a torso here, an arm there, in the course of business.

The Rockland detectives had dismissed the possibility of any connection between Zelenin and the Russian mob, or of organized crime's involvement at all. Only the method had been Russian, they concluded.

Vladimir Zelenin had chosen to dissect Yakov Gluzman, Colantonio learned, because he hadn't been resourceful enough to find a gun, his first choice of weapon. Unaware of the case with which New Yorkers bought firearms in states such as Virginia, or on street corners in Brooklyn and upper Manhattan, the illegal immigrant had given up finding a gun and simply walked into the Home Depot store in nearby Paramus, New Jersey, where he purchased an ax, a hatchet, and a hacksaw. Zelenin never thought twice about slicing

Yakov Gluzman up. It would be easier to get the large body out of his apartment, which he had decided would be the most reasonable place to kill Yakov. Dissecting his victim would greatly ease in the disposal of the body.

He hadn't bought any Henckel knives, however.

Through their interpreters, the detectives had learned that Zelenin was born and raised in Kyrgyzstan, next to the old Soviet republic of Kazakhstan, several thousand miles southeast of Moscow, on the border of China near Pakistan. Kyrgyzstan was an isolated province, known primarily for its oil base, and Zelenin was one of only a few Jews there. It was predominantly Muslim, like Kazakhstan, and both had a reputation for anti-Semitism beyond that of even Moscow, more active than passive in its treatment of Jews. Zelenin had graduated from the state university, and had even earned a master's degree in physics. But he'd been fired as a teacher, he said, because of union activities, and had been able to find work only as a janitor.

In December 1993, Zelenin's wife had been shot and killed at the currency exchange office where she worked, leaving the man a confused single father of their two boys, who were then twelve and ten. With his parents' help, Zelenin had somehow managed to survive, but he spent his waking hours devising a plan to escape the crumbling republic, and to get to the U.S., where he had some Russian acquaintances. Finally, he'd fled, lacking papers, and gone to the U.S., settling temporarily in Brooklyn with a cousin, Gregory Kogan, before sending for his sons, who were reunited with their father in 1994.

Zelenin had attempted to gain permanent residency in the U.S., and lied, successfully, to the Immigration

and Naturalization Service (INS) by claiming to seek
political asylum from Kyrgyzstan. He'd told the immigration
authorities that his wife had been murdered in an
anti-Semitic incident, when in truth she had simply been
another crime victim in the desperate former Soviet
republic. This the detectives discovered after several
interviews with the prisoner, once he had warmed to
the American interrogators and realized that his case
was hopeless.

In the pressure cooker life that is the immigrant's fate
in a country where he speaks little of the native tongue
and has limited financial resources, Zelenin had somehow functioned nevertheless and, through Kogan, met
Rita Gluzman, who was their mutual cousin. She offered
Zelenin a job as a handyman at ECI in 1994, just as he
was beginning to have great difficulty with Kogan, who
knew of his deceit with INS. Zelenin testified that Kogan
was demanding money from him, threatening to turn
him in to the authorities if the illegal refugee didn't
pay him. So Zelenin left Brooklyn for East Rutherford
and soon Rita found him an apartment in Fair Lawn,
where her mother had lived. Zelenin took his two sons
to New Jersey and enrolled the boys in school, hoping
to start a better life for them. Kogan continued his
threats, but Zelenin stalled his blackmailing cousin from
carrying through and reporting him to INS by promising to pay him at some point.

Zelenin had had something of an epiphany when
he'd been captured. Rita, he said, had gotten him into
this mess. He hadn't wanted to kill Yakov Gluzman, but
she'd forced him into cooperating with her because
Yakov was going to leave her, and if he did ECI would
be devastated financially, leaving Zelenin in financial
jeopardy once more. He and his sons would be deported, and would face certain death back home in

Kyrgyzstan. This time, his Jewishness would get him. He
could not envision facing this. He had thought he and
his sons were safe in the United States—until Rita's
threat.

The two of them had begun talking about killing
Yakov in February 1996, when Rita approached him
during the day at ECI. At first Zelenin told her she
was crazy, that she would never get away with it, while
thinking to himself, why in the world is she involving
me in this monstrosity? I can't kill Yakov!

The detectives then learned why their prisoner was
especially repulsed at the prospect of doing this dirty
deed for his boss. Zelenin testified that Yakov had
loaned him $2,000 the previous fall in order to pay
Gregory Kogan. The biologist had sympathized with
the plight of his wife's cousin, having emigrated from
elsewhere himself. Zelenin had repaid $1,900 to Yakov
by February 1996. This grated at the prisoner. Intimidated by Kogan, the man he'd once trusted, Zelenin
was able to pay the extortion demand only because of
Yakov, the man he'd come to like, and now Rita was
insisting he kill his benefactor.

Vladimir Zelenin had a conflicted mind and heart,
but his desperation in protecting himself and his sons
pushed him over the edge and he'd gone along with
Rita Gluzman, laying a trap for Yakov when he'd come
home from Lederle and killing, then dismembering,
the one man he'd known in the U.S. who had displayed
kindness to him.

At the same time, having had almost four weeks to
examine all the characters involved in the brutal murder
case, the detectives and DA had looked very carefully
at what they had learned about Rita Gluzman. They

sought a psychological profile of the woman that might explain her actions.

Steve Colantonio had summed up Rita Gluzman after one meeting. "She was a control freak, I could tell at the beginning. I knew that for certain."

It hadn't taken the seasoned detective long to figure out what had happened in Pearl River between Rita and Yakov the previous Saturday night. Experience teaches homicide detectives where to look first after the strange unnatural death of a married person, and which person is most likely to have killed somebody. It rarely took genius to determine the nearest and dearest were most culpable, and detectives' hunches are borne out by crime statistics.

Zelenin's confession had been convincing enough, especially when he implicated Rita Gluzman as the catalyst of the murder, and detailed to the investigators how desperate he'd been and why he had been so vulnerable to his cousin's demands. Colantonio had sensed Sunday evening Gluzman had been involved, he just hadn't known to what degree. Because Zelenin had no apparent motive to kill Yakov Gluzman, the two men were almost like ships passing in the night, he thought. Once he'd eliminated the possibility of a sexual relationship, he concentrated on the money, and Rita's desire to have things her way at all times. He concluded she was an obsessive and highly intelligent person, who had gone beyond the limit in trying to save a fractured marriage, only because she couldn't see it end due to the work of someone else.

So, Colantonio figured, she's just a cold, controlling person who decided to kill her husband after losing her influence over him, and that control had been all that mattered to Rita. She could have had most of the family's money without a problem: Yakov had tendered a generous settlement offer to Rita, more than half the couple's $1.5 million fortune, if she'd agree to a divorce. Sex was no longer a significant part of Yakov and Rita's relationship, despite their assignations during the separation at Yakov's apartment. Though she was attractive and maintained her appearance, sex was not the chief concern in Rita's daily life. Control was. And she'd clearly lost whatever of it she had over her husband after he refused to reconcile their marriage. Yakov's relationship with Raisa Korenblit had angered Rita to the point of distraction, and her estranged husband had discussed with his friends the possibility of relocating to Israel or Boston, both for a fresh start and to get away from Rita.

With Yakov dead, Rita would get everything in the couple's estate, too, including complete control of ECI. There would be no cash-flow problems, no disputes with anybody wishing to look at the company's books, and her lifestyle would be unhindered.

The detectives realized Rita Gluzman was not a professional criminal. She was very bright, scholarly, with a degree in chemical engineering. Like most intelligent amateurs who'd set out to commit a serious crime, she'd left an abundance of evidence in her wake, a trail she hadn't even been aware of. Buying the bandages at CVS was among her mistakes, Colantonio and Tom Hoffmann knew. They looked for others.

Because of her intelligence and many accomplishments, Rita's level of self-confidence was high, and she was no stranger to hard work in solving problems, whether it was getting Yakov out of the Soviet Union, establishing herself in the United States, or building ECI, which had been her idea, into a multimillion dollar company that could only grow larger.

* * *

In the absence of physical evidence, the hunch of a veteran detective and the suspicions of every investigator in two states, simply isn't enough to charge somebody with murder, let alone win conviction against them in a court of law, at least not in the United States and certainly not in the state of New York. Colantonio knew he had to find absolute proof of Rita's presence inside the Pearl River apartment the night Zelenin claimed they both killed Yakov Gluzman there. He and the other members of the government task force set out to find the home-run evidence that would convince a jury Rita Gluzman was guilty.

The business card Carlos Rodriguez found behind the dryer in Rita's garage proved valuable. Joe Mullen, whose card it was, was a respected longtime private investigator in New York City who specialized both in background research in business and in matrimonial work. An ex-New York City detective, Mullen had worked for a number of rich and famous clients, including Donald Trump. When the detectives interviewed the older Mullen, they learned that Rita had tried to hire him the previous September. She'd asked him for help in "saving her marriage," Mullen told them, and in "saving an American family," a term others who knew Rita Gluzman said she used. Saving an American family had a nice, urgent ring to it. But Mullen had declined to do any further work for Rita after she'd asked about his services apart from surveillance: did he kill people? Did he know of anyone who did? Or so she'd seemed to suggest, Mullen told them. After Rita had said she merely wanted to prevent Raisa Korenblit from entering the country, the established private detective's defenses had been raised. He'd referred her, before she told him about wanting to do harm to anybody, to a couple of other private detectives and suggested she find somebody in Israel if she wanted her husband's girlfriend tailed. All in all though, he would wait to be subpoenaed for Rita Gluzman's trial to tell them more about his erstwhile client. Mullen had gotten a bad feeling about Gluzman. She had seemed to him the sort of client whose amateurism would jeopardize his established business.

Other parts of Vladimir Zelenin's story were checking out. A microcassette recorder with a recent tape of Yakov Gluzman's phone conversations was found in the front seat of the blue Taurus, and the detectives traced the recorder to a spot where it had been placed behind the refrigerator in Yakov's apartment. Joe Mullen had told them of Rita's desire to check an apartment for listening devices. He had told her about using a "sweep" crew, two young guys from Queens who could find listening devices if they were hidden. The detectives found the technicians from the telephone number in the 718 area code Rodriguez had found on Mullen's card. They learned that Rita Gluzman had asked the two men to *install* a bug, not find one, in an apartment, and they had visited what they believed was the woman's place in Pearl River. They'd thought it was her apartment because she had the key and had let the two men in to plant a tape recorder behind her refrigerator. She had told them she wanted to tape her own calls because she was being harassed, and had paid them for their trouble with a check.

The two men identified the recorder from Zelenin's car as the one they had sold to Rita.

* * *

The plate was getting full, as far as Cathy Seibel and Lou Valvo were concerned, but they needed more. There would be no help at the trial from the general forensic evidence used in most murder cases, such as hair fibers or DNA. It was no secret that Yakov and Rita Gluzman had retained a sex life together even after Yakov had moved out of the family home. Rita's hair, even her blood, would not be unexpected at his apartment. The prosecution couldn't prove burglary, robbery, or even ordinary breaking-and-entering charges against Rita either: only her dead husband could ascertain whether he had willingly given her the key to the Pearl River apartment.

Rita's divorce attorney, Barry Croland, was respected throughout the matrimonial bar in the state of New Jersey. While he had recommended Joe Mullen to his client in late 1995, Croland was prohibited by client/attorney privilege from discussing any of Rita's intentions or motives, or even whether he believed she had contributed to her husband's death. The attorney willingly shared with the law enforcement team his filings and correspondence with Yakov on Rita's behalf, but he, too, would need to be subpoenaed in order to tell anything more, assuming the credible and generally beyond-reproach Croland could.

The prosecutors and detectives learned of Rita Gluzman's affinity for Henckel knives, the quality kitchen cutlery that was a more expensive choice of flatware than the run-of-the-mill knives most would buy. Rita loved Henckels. There was a set in the Upper Saddle River home. Henckel knives had been found in Zelenin's Taurus in East Rutherford. A set of recently purchased Henckel knives was found in Rita Gluzman's Taurus when she was discovered at Cold Spring Harbor. A piece of a Henckel knife was found inside Yakov Gluzman's arm, its tip broken apparently while Zelenin and his accomplice were dissecting their victim. But most importantly, one of the knives from Rita's home block was missing.

After interviewing Yakov's co-workers at Lederle Labs and those who remembered the biologist from his days at Cold Spring Harbor Labs on Long Island, Deirdre Daly and Cathy Seibel reached the same conclusions Steve Colantonio and Lou Valvo had: Yakov Gluzman was sincerely liked, and unusually well respected, by nearly everyone he'd worked with in his nineteen years in the U.S. Many of the witnesses interviewed expressed reservations about Rita: she was just a little too shrill and not the most pleasant woman they'd known. Fortunately for Rita, unpopularity wasn't a crime, but the repeated stories of frequent quarrels with her husband, or her materialistic, new-money ways, or reports of her lack of spirituality, hounded the investigators, who early on looked for reasons to refute her apparent involvement as they challenged all assumptions looking into Yakov's death. As one investigator had commented, when everything points in one direction, start looking the other way. But the trail always led back to Rita, a widow who hadn't spent a great deal of time grieving, and searches for others with a motive to kill Yakov had turned up empty.

There was also the issue of Yakov's love life after he had separated from Rita. Experiencing life as a bachelor for the first time since the 1960s, and for the first time ever in the United States, Yasha Gluzman had found he was popular with women, and they had seemed attracted to the scientist constantly in his sixteen months as a bachelor. Jake Szpicek and Tom Hoffmann discovered that a woman rumored to be involved with the scientist had in fact been the last person to see Yakov Gluzman alive, at 11:30 Saturday evening, as the two left the Lederle campus together where they were colleagues. The woman had been devastated at learning of her friend Yasha's brutal killing, sobbing to the detectives who learned of her liaison with her fellow biologist. Moreover, the woman was married, with children, and the public rumor of an office romance with Yakov could destroy her. As a material witness, the Lederle co-worker would most likely be called to testify in court. Could she handle that? the DA discreetly inquired. Without hesitation, the co-worker agreed.

Whoever had killed Yakov Gluzman with Vladimir Zelenin had upset the equilibrium of a number of lives. The detectives and prosecutors were determined that their prime suspect, Rita Gluzman, would be dealt with as thoroughly as possible.

In addition, there was the attempted shakedown of Yakov's father in Israel. At first, the authorities in Tel Aviv had been reluctant to cooperate with the Americans, shocked as everybody else at the tragedy of Yakov Gluzman's death and not yet completely aware of all the facets of the extortion plot that had been attempted against Chaim Gluzman. Michael Gluzman prodded the police in Hadera to do everything possible to ensure justice for his older brother and prison for whoever had killed him. Michael Gluzman had few doubts that Rita had killed Yakov.

The private eyes who had come forward to Hadera police were being interviewed there. But, in general, no one in Israel wished to be associated with the case of brutal homicide such as the one that had taken place outside their territory, especially since there was little any of the Israeli police could do. They seemed unwilling to make any aggressive investigation on their own.

Jake Szpicek stepped in, aided by his friend Hilda Kogut, the FBI special agent who had come into the case during the early stages of the investigation. Kogut worked out of an airplane hangar in upstate Newburgh that was home to the FBI's exurban office west of the Hudson. Drug smugglers, kidnappers, mob traffic, whatever moved through the tiny area near West Point where Kogut was stationed, was the usual game for Bureau matters there. This was different: a sickening homicide of someone who tried to save lives by preventing cancer.

Szpicek and Kogut realized they would have to go to Israel before Rita Gluzman's trial if they were to get to the bottom of the extortion attempt against Chaim Gluzman and find a connection to Rita. If they proved she was also plotting to shake down her father-in-law, or threatening the frail man in order to get at Yakov, the statements of those she had hired overseas would be invaluable to the prosecution in showing a pattern of harassment that led, ultimately, to killing her husband after all else had failed.

Eleven

Rita Gluzman's attorney Mike Rosen was a prominent criminal defense attorney in Manhattan, one of the best trial lawyers in New York and, for that matter, in the United States. When *Town and Country Magazine* had named the Brooklyn Law almunus one of the hundred best criminal lawyers in America in 1986, he had been overjoyed to be included on the same list as his hero, Edward Bennett Williams. Rosen felt he had finally won recognition as one of the elite members of the criminal bar anywhere, a heavy-hitter. He was expensive talent.

Rosen had spent years practicing with the legendary Roy Cohn at Saxe Bacon & Bolan, where he was the courtroom counterpart at the firm to Cohn's rainmaker. Saxe Bacon represented the top echelon of New York's wealthy—and colorful—movers and shakers, and Rosen learned early on how to handle the toughest of clients and function in the most competitive hallways of the law. After Cohn's death in 1987, the firm disbanded

and most of its lawyers went to other leading Manhattan
law firms. Rosen began practice anew with several colleagues from Saxe, and launched a practice downtown.

Rita Gluzman had found him almost by accident. Her
lawyer at ECI's outside law firm had called Mike Davis,
an old law school friend, late on the Friday afternoon
after Rita's arrest in Cold Spring Harbor. Davis' and
Rosen's association dated back to their years together
with Roy Cohn. Davis was finishing an important case
in the office, and asked Rosen, who was running out to
a dinner date, if he would instead make a jail appearance
for his friend's client, a woman who was in trouble on
Long Island. Rosen sped to Woodbury and shortly after
meeting the frightened widow he had taken up her
cause. The lawyer was slighty familiar with the death of
Yakov Gluzman, having read briefly about the crime in
the paper earlier that week.

Rosen had established his reputation representing
some of the least popular of New York's high-powered
people, including reputed mobsters such as Thomas
Gambino, a rumored godfather for whom he won acquittal so successfully in the late 1980s that members of the
jury questioned the government's indictment of Gambino
in a note the foreman sent to the judge during the trial.
When John Gotti, one of the most famous of New York's
underworld, had been tried and convicted in 1991 on
racketeering charges that would send him away for life,
Rosen had gotten Gambino, a co-defendant, acquitted.
In addition to his prominent organized crime clientele,
it seemed to Rosen that every few years he'd be called to
defend a woman accused in a sensational murder: Rita
Gluzman's was the attorney's third headline case in ten
years involving a wife or daughter accused of killing their
husband or father for money.

From his perch at 17 Battery Place, facing the Hudson

River and the Statue of Liberty, Rosen and his firm commanded retainers from some of Manhattan's prominent moneyed elite. The lawyer was accustomed to walking around his office wearing a photographer's flak jacket over a tailored Paul Stuart shirt and tie, the better to carry gear around during a typically hectic day as he chain-smoked Parliament Lights. While he might earn a respectable sum defending Rita Gluzman, it would be pale in comparison to the money Rosen received from some of his bigger clients. But the lawyer liked the fight, the challenge of making the government prove its case against an unpopular client. He could do so while usually arguing the pertinent laws and facts of a case, rarely if ever needing to exploit more emotional issues. Rosen enjoyed the law, with its many complexities and issues. When he was fresh out of law school in the 1960s, Rosen hadn't been anxious to go to Vietnam and had gone to work for the U.S. Attorney's Office in Brooklyn where, in a touch of irony, the federal prosecutor assigned him to pursue draft dodgers who had used fraud to avoid going into the army. While he respected the law and the constitution, Rosen was constantly skeptical of the power of the government and its frequent intrusions, as he judged them, into the lives of ordinary citizens. This philosophy had drawn him along with Mike Davis to Rita Gluzman.

With apparently no conclusive direct forensic evidence or independent eyewitness placing his client at the crime scene, or involved at all in the murder for that matter, Rosen was unconvinced of the government's accusations against Rita, thought the prosecutors were overreaching, and demanded Daly and Seibel prove their case. The venue was especially bothersome to the veteran lawyer: selecting a jury in federal court gave him little leeway in choosing its members, owing to the

difference in voir dire. There were far fewer exclusion-
ary challenges available to the defense, and the government would enjoy the luxury of introducing Zelenin's
testimony, inadmissable in state court, and that alone
could destroy his client. Rosen felt he would easily exon-
erate Rita Gluzman if she were on trial in Rockland or
another local court.

Rosen realized that, with his client facing life imprisonment if she were convicted, he and Davis would have
to work double-time in the six or so months until the
trial to ensure a maximum defense, especially since the
novelty of the federal charge against Rita Gluzman was
uncharted territory. The lawyer felt he could use assis-
tance from someone with trial experience similar to his
own, so he reached out to a longtime criminal defender
he respected and trusted, Lawrence Hochheiser, who
Rosen knew had won many acquittals over twenty-five
years for clients accused of violent crimes, including a
reputed member of the violent Westies gang.

Larry Hochheiser was the man people in New York
City called when they were in serious trouble, and was
one of perhaps three criminal trial lawyers in New York
whose competence Rosen respected completely. Hochheiser had saved many a life sentence for his clients
through the years, and had seen some of them walk free
with greater cases against them than the U.S. Attorney
seemed to have for Rita Gluzman. The lawyer could
inject reasonable doubt into the tightest of cases the
government had made against his clients, who paid him
handsomely for the privilege of his counsel and bulldog
manner at the defense table. Rosen sensed his friend
would prove to be great help in acquitting Rita. Hochheiser agreed to join the defense.

Because the bulk of the government's case against Rita Gluzman would hinge on Zelenin's testimony, Rosen and Hochheiser knew they'd have to attack the confessed murderer on the witness stand, impeach his credibility, and show the jury that whatever motive Rita's cousin had for testifying against her so agreeably—after all, he was cooperative, not a hostile witness—would convince the twelve people who would decide Rita's fate that the prosecutors had somehow railroaded her in the absence of other suspects.

Neither Rosen nor Hochheiser came cheaply; the demand for their expert services was great enough to warrant large fees for their time. Ilan Gluzman had agreed to help pay his mother's lawyers with money from Yakov's insurance policies in which he was sole beneficiary. The young man had been caught in a dilemma of Hobson's choice proportions: he'd lost his father in a brutal murder and his mother, who was also his only other close relative, was on trial for the crime. He wanted to believe she was not involved with Zelenin, and Ilan chose not to abandon his mother.

No matter how much money the defendant had at her disposal, it would seem paltry next to the combined budget of the United States government. Also, regardless of the reputations of Mike Rosen, Mike Davis, and Larry Hochheiser, the prosecutors had to be considered a prohibitive favorite as they held the potential trump card in Vladimir Zelenin. No law firm could match the collective resources of the U.S. Attorney, the FBI, BCI, the Rockland County DA, the Orangetown PD, and other contributing government entities.

* * *

Deirdre Daly had run the Southern District's White Plains office for two and a half years, spending the majority of her time prosecuting racketeering, murder, and narcotics crimes in addition to the ordinary white-collar crime, tax evasion, and corruption cases that occurred within the northern counties. There was plenty of organized crime activity in the sprawling suburban district to keep the prosecutor and her staff of thirteen assistants busy, from Poughkeepsie in the north to Elmsford and White Plains closer to the office. The straight-laced Daly was a product of Dartmouth and Georgetown Law, and, after her federal clerkship, had spent her entire eleven-year career as a prosecutor with the U.S. Attorney. Rudolph Giuliani had hired her to work in the Manhattan office during the active years of the 1980s mob and Wall Street crime wave that had established Giuliani's prominence as a no-nonsense prosecutor.

Daly's assistant, Cathy Seibel, who was chosen to lead the government's prosecution of Rita Gluzman, was a native of Long Island and another Ivy League graduate, who'd won her law degree magna cum laude at Fordham, known for its many alumni both in the government and in the judiciary. Seibel also had spent her entire career as a federal prosecutor, having begun not long after Daly in the Manhattan office in the 1980s, where she established herself by working long hours in the government's case that had convicted hotel magnate Leona Helmsley of tax fraud and sent her to a federal penitentiary.

Both Daly and Seibel had preferred to wear the "white hats" working for the justice department offered them, as Mike Bongiorno and Lou Valvo enjoyed being DAs. The two women enjoyed their work, and neither of the professional prosecutors had regrets about their choice to enforce the government's stance toward the law and not defendants'. A month after the discovery of Yakov Gluzman's dissected body, Rosen and Hochheiser were as passionate about the lack of proof the government had of Rita Gluzman's participation in her husband's death, as Daly and Seibel were adamant about her complicity.

Twelve

Over the summer, the Rockland detectives catalogued the growing evidence collection, several hundred pieces, for Seibel's office, painstakingly organizing phone bills, Federal Express airbills, canceled checks, and the settlement offer Rita Gluzman had rejected, among other paperwork. Steve Colantonio had found the ticket from LaGuardia airport proving Gluzman's short presence there late on the Sunday her husband's remains were found. There was everything but blood showing Rita's presence at the Pearl River apartment at some point prior to Yakov's death. They were locked in the Quarropas evidence room, along with the ax and hatchet found with Zelenin and the set of Henckel knives from the Taurus.

Gluzman had spent four months at the Valhalla jail, frustrated in her attempts to win release on bail before trial even though her attorneys had offered every asset she owned as bond. By late September, her attorneys were frustrated, too, as the strict visitation privileges at Valhalla limited Rosen's and Hochheiser's interaction with their client, who faced life imprisonment, and the lawyers needed time with her to plan their defense. Again, they asked for a bail hearing, and one was granted for October 7.

The quiet, courtly judge who was assigned to preside over the Gluzman case was second-generation jurist Barrington Parker, Jr., an Ivy Leaguer from Yale and Yale Law whose father was a part of the Washington, D.C., legal establishment in the 1960s. With Rita's trial three months away, Parker reviewed Hochheiser's motion and heard Rita Gluzman's plea for bail.

"Everything I love and everything I have is in this country," Rita said, nearly shouting, the months of imprisonment showing their effect on the woman. "I have to show my son, my family, my people that I am innocent.

"I am going to prove I am not guilty, or I am going to die," she continued. "That's it. There's nothing else."

Parker was unmoved. The judge wasn't certain whether his trial would have its suspect present, and with little fanfare he denied Rita's request, citing the flight risk. Hochheiser was flustered, but returned to his office to work on the case while Gluzman was remanded to Valhalla. They would have to wait until January to see if Rita would ever again walk in the outside world.

Deirdre Daly and Mike Bongiorno decided that a part of the investigation would be a trip to Israel by the detectives, to interview David Rom, who was now a material witness in an American homicide case, and the victim's brother and father, Michael and Chaim Gluzman, who would make plans later to attend Rita's trial. Raisa Korenblit had indicated she would come to the U.S. to testify. Rom would not. They had to get his statement personally. Also the Israeli authorities were still not cooperating fully with the American investigation. As the summer drew to a close, and the trial lay ahead, it was left to Cathy Seibel and Lou Valvo to plan the trip, which would be essential in proving the extortion charge in Rita Gluzman's indictment, and possibly the conspiracy count as well.

The senior prosecutors decided FBI Special Agent Hilda Kogut, Rockland DA Senior Detective Steve Colantonio, and Orangetown Detective Tom Hoffmann would go to interview Rom and the Gluzman family in late October. There was enough money available to pay for the FBI agent, the DA's detective, and the local investigator to go. Colantonio reminded them of Jake Szpicek's usefulness, and suggested it would be only prudent to have the Rockland deputy sheriff—a criminal investigator and someone who spoke the native tongue of the country where they would travel—accompany them. The only problem was the budget. Deirdre Daly made a special request to James F. Kralik, the Rockland Sheriff, to include Szpicek in the investigation team to Israel. Szpicek was, after all, the essential hook to the investigators' contact with local authorities in Hadera, Tel Aviv, and Jerusalem, and was the only one of the crew who could introduce the American detectives to the necessary supervisors who could open doors. The sheriff approved Jake's participation after learning of the importance of one of his deputies to the U.S. Attorney.

* * *

Colantonio, Kogut, and Hoffmann had never been to Israel. Each was excited to visit, though the circumstances of their mission dampened some of the joy the trip ordinarily would have had for them. Szpicek reassured his colleagues that all would run smoothly.

As their flight touched down, Szpicek told his three companions to wait until everyone else had deplaned and boarded the buses waiting for passengers on the tarmac. Shortly after the 396 others got on the standard airport buses, a caravan of cars pulled alongside the 747. A police car stopped in front of them, and Szpicek smiled as he introduced his colleagues to the commanders of the Tel Aviv police department, including Superintendents Shimon Tzubery and Isaac Norber, who had arranged the escort. From there, the four were sped to Shinbet headquarters a short distance from the airport. Kogut, Colantonio, and Hoffmann spent the day looking through Israeli police files, then decided to head to the Hilton, where the U.S. travel agency had booked them at its government rate. But Szpicek had another surprise for his colleagues: the more spacious and comfortable Ramada nearby, which charged a rate lower than the stateside agency had found. The next day, Eton Chanover, a representative of the Israeli government, and Brigadier General Yosi Setbon, chief of Israel's police investigative divisions, met with the Americans to map out a strategy for their investigation.

After meeting with Interpol's representatives, the four Americans spent six days in Tel Aviv and Hadera, where they interviewed Michael and Chaim Gluzman, Raisa Korenblit, and then David Rom and Benny Lefkowitz, the private investigators who by prior arrangement with

Deirdre Daly had consented to video testimony concerning Rita Gluzman and her use of their services. Tzubery and General Assaf Hefetz, Israel's Police Commissioner who was based in Jerusalem and was Szpicek's *kibbutz* buddy, had persuaded the witnesses to share anything asked of them with the Americans after the commanders had met again with Jake Szpicek. Complying with discovery and trial rules, Daly had informed Larry Hochheiser of the prosecution's trip to Israel and the interview with Rom. Hochheiser had consented and had several questions of his own for the investigator who had purportedly taken the photos of Yakov Gluzman with Raisa Korenblit.

At the end of the week-long trip, Kogut, Hoffmann, Colantonio, and Szpicek were ready to return to New York and report to Seibel and Valvo. They had a videotaped interview of Rom, as well as interviews with Yakov Gluzman's family, the people who were most interested in the justice process as it related to the killer or killers of Yakov Gluzman. Before leaving, Szpicek once again demonstrated his hospitality, casually walking into the government office building in Tel Aviv and calling his friend Eton Chanover, who introduced them to Shimon Peres, the Israeli Foreign Minister, in Peres' private office. Peres exchanged stories with the American investigators, who told one of the most powerful officials in the Middle East how cooperative Israel's authorities had been with them as they sought justice for one of the better scientists his country had produced. Israel's important law enforcement officials had lent the Rockland contingent the full support of their offices. It now remained for Daly, Seibel, and Valvo to use as much of the information the investigators had learned in Israel in their case against Rita Gluzman.

                        * * *

As the months leading to Rita Gluzman's trial progressed, Seibel and her staff were examining additional
counts with which they'd charge her. When the investigative team returned from its Israeli trip in November,
Seibel and Daly listened to Rom's interview and the
statements of Chaim and Michael Gluzman, and the
U.S. Attorney superceded the previous indictment of
Rita, including the new charge of extortion. Between the
detectives' suspicions that Rita had written the letters to
Chaim Gluzman and the odd coincidence that one of
the photos taken by Benny Lefkowitz had surfaced in
the police investigation in the contents of the extortion
letter, as well as the revelation that Rita Gluzman had
traveled to Israel on business twice in 1995 just before
the letters were mailed, Seibel believed the government
had more than ample cause to think Rita was the extortionist.

The government had until thirty days before the trial's
opening, now scheduled for January 6, 1997, to add
charges, to supercede a previous indictment. By early
December, the prosecutors had completed their analysis
of the investigator's collected statements and evidence,
and the case of U.S. v. Rita Gluzman now charged Yakov
Gluzman's widow with conspiracy to commit murder,
extortion, and interstate domestic violence resulting in
death, along with two minor charges, illegal interception of oral communications and use of a device to
intercept oral comunications.

On December 16, jury selection was held in Judge
Parker's courtroom. By the end of the day, eight men
and four women had been selected to hear a case of
brutal murder and dismemberment and decide the fate
of a forty-eight-year-old widow charged with master-

minding her husband's death. One potential juror was excused by Parker as she began to get ill when the crime was described. Parker was compassionate, then completed the selection process by adding six alternates, including five women.

The holiday season is a miserable time for anybody to be in jail. Rita Gluzman consoled herself by receiving her son, sister, and mother at Valhalla, and by reading as much as she could of Rosen's and Hochheiser's plans for her defense.

Thirteen

A packed courtroom greeted Rita Gluzman and her lawyers Mike Rosen and Larry Hochheiser the morning of January 6, 1997. The case of U.S. v. Gluzman was the most sensational trial to hit White Plains in years, and was the most prominent case to be heard in the short history of the Quarropas Street Federal Building and Courthouse since its completion three years earlier.

At the government's table, Deirdre Daly, Cathy Seibel, and Lou Valvo organized their time-line for the trial, which, Parker had told them, to expect to last five weeks. Behind the prosecutors, Steve Colantonio, Jake Szpicek, and Tom Hoffmann exchanged glances with Hilda Kogut and Joe Higgins. All were anxious to see how Valvo and Seibel performed with the details of their investigation.

There were no protesters outside on the chilly winter day chanting "Justice for Rita," and no Court TV analysts or guest lawyers debating the uniqueness of her indictment under the Federal Crime Bill's Violence Against Women statute, though some reporters wondered whether the absence of physical evidence placing her at the crime scene the night of her husband's murder would prove crucial to her defense. Because this was a federal trial, cameras were forbidden in the courtroom.

Only one of the jurors selected the previous month had had to declare hardship, after his house burned down over the holidays. Judge Parker deemed that a reasonable cause to be excused. Mike Rosen and Larry Hochheiser were satisfied with the twelve men and women chosen, sensing some skepticism toward the government on the part of several of the eight men on the jury. Rita Gluzman's case called for many of those present to be skeptical of the government's intentions in order for her to win acquittal.

With no corroboration of his testimony needed in federal court, Vladimir Zelenin's statements would carry greater weight than they would have had the trial been in Rockland. The widow Gluzman, still had no alibi for her whereabouts the Saturday night of her husband's murder.

Michael Gluzman and his parents had flown in from Israel, as had Raisa Korenblit, who sat apart from the Gluzmans. Michael would be escorted outside while the first of the witnesses testified so his own testimony would not be tainted. A crowd of Yakov's co-workers from Lederle sat impassively as they waited to see how his widow fared. Rita's sister, Mariann Rabinowitz, and her mother, Paula Shapiro, sat behind the defense table nervously.

Judge Parker greeted the jurors and gave them a

preview of the nature of the trial laying ahead. They wouldn't be sequestered, but needed to eliminate reading the newspapers for a few weeks. As it was the heart of the professional football season's playoffs, a few men groaned, but were reassured the sports section would be acceptable reading. Judge Parker then read his standard instructions concerning procedure and communication during trial, and the case of U.S. v. Rita Gluzman opened officially nearing 10 A.M. on Monday, January 6, 1997, following nearly nine months of preparation by the state and federal prosecutors after the gruesome murder of Dr. Yakov Gluzman.

Opening arguments by attorneys set the tone for most trials, and a case can be established immediately with an effective opening. This Cathy Seibel had decided to do, to get immediately to the root of the government's case against Rita Gluzman.

The assistant U.S. Attorney stood and spoke.

"This is a case about a brutal, coldblooded murder, a murder that this defendant set in motion, this defendant planned, this defendant committed, and this defendant attempted to cover up. It is the murder of Yakov Gluzman, the defendant's husband.

"Rita Gluzman committed this horrendous crime because her husband had moved out, filed for divorce, and found a girlfriend in Israel. The defendant was angry, jealous, and desperately afraid that without her husband and his money, she would lose her business and her comfortable lifestyle. So she wiretapped the phone in her husband's apartment. She sent anonymous threatening letters to her husband and his father demanding large sums of money, and when neither of these crimes stopped her husband from going through with the divorce, she turned to the most monstrous crime of all: murder.

"She recruited her cousin, a recent Russian immigrant, a man who spoke little English, and was entirely dependent on her for his money, his job, his car, and his home. Then on the night of April 6th of last year, armed with axes, the defendant and her cousin lay in wait in her husband's apartment, and when Yakov Gluzman came through his door, they attacked him with those axes and killed him. Later, the cousin dismembered the victim's body while the defendant cleaned the blood that had been spilled."

There was little ambiguity in Cathy Seibel's statement to the jury, and the prosecutor delivered her comments confidently, succinctly, and with no hesitation.

Seibel continued. "After I review what the government expects the evidence to show, I will describe the various crimes charged in the indictment. So what will the evidence show?

"It will show that the defendant and Yakov Gluzman, who were born in the Soviet Union, had been married for twenty-six years. When they were young, the defendant had struggled to get her husband permission to leave Russia. They and their son, Ilan, eventually settled in the United States. Her husband, Yakov Gluzman, worked as a molecular biologist doing cancer research, and the defendant worked in the field of chemistry. In the late eighties, they started a company called ECI Technology, which specialized in electroplating equipment. Yakov Gluzman and the defendant co-owned the company. The defendant was president of ECI and worked there full-time. While Yakov helped out with ECI, he worked full-time elsewhere. At the time of his death he worked in Lederle Labs, in Pearl River, New York, in Rockland County. ECI was located in East Rutherford, New Jersey, in Bergen County, right next to

Rockland, and the Gluzman home was also in Bergen County, in Upper Saddle River.

"The evidence will show that the Gluzmans had marital problems. Finally, Yakov Gluzman moved out of the family home in early 1995 and took a small apartment in Pearl River, near his work. Through his lawyer, he tried to negotiate a property settlement with the defendant, but when she rejected the agreement, he filed for divorce. He also found a new woman in his life, Raisa Korenblit, who lived in Israel, as did Yakov Gluzman's brother and parents. When the defendant learned about Yakov's relationship with Raisa, she was furious and became obsessed with breaking up their relationship even though she and Yakov were separated and living apart. The evidence will show that in fall 1995, the defendant hired a private investigator and asked him to try to keep Raisa Korenblit out of the United States, saying that Raisa was trying to break up an American family, a family that in reality had already been broken up.

"The evidence will also show that in the fall of 1995, the defendant hired a security expert to go to Yakov Gluzman's apartment with her. The defendant had a key to the apartment. She lied and told the security man it was her own apartment and that she wanted him to search it for listening devices and bugs. What she wanted was information about her husband's phone lines, and equipment she could use to secretly record her husband's calls. You'll learn that once the defendant got that information and equipment, she hid a small micro-cassette recorder behind the refrigerator in Yakov Gluzman's kitchen and illegally taped his telephone conversations and messages. You'll see the equipment she used and the tapes she made."

Seibel explained the ramifications of Rita's unlawful

wiretapping, leading the jury chronologically through late 1995.

"The evidence will also show that Rita Gluzman committed another crime arising out of anger at her husband, her jealousy of his relationship with Raisa Korenblit, and the fear that the divorce would deprive her of the company and her lifestyle. In September of 1995, the defendant traveled to Israel. It was a business trip, but it had another purpose as well. Knowing that Yakov Gluzman was also in Israel at the time, the defendant hired an Israeli private investigator named David Rom, and paid him to gather information about Raisa Korenblit, the woman Yakov Gluzman had been seeing. David Rom, in turn, hired another private investigator, Benny Lefkowitz, who took pictures of Raisa and Yakov together and gave the pictures, along with other information, to David Rom."

As Seibel outlined the extortion case, in sequence with the wiretap and murder charge, the jurors realized they were hearing a number of unseemly things about the woman seated at the defense table.

"The evidence will also show that as 1995 ended and 1996 began, Rita Gluzman was becoming more and more desperate. The divorce case was proceeding and the defendant and her husband were battling over money and over control of ECI. The defendant was panicked at the thought of losing her husband to Raisa, losing the lifestyle her husband's substantial income had supported, and losing the company that she headed and that paid for so much. That winter, the defendant contacted another private investigator, seeking his help in preventing Raisa Korenblit from coming to the United States. The defendant suggested that the private investigator plant cocaine on Raisa and have her arrested, and that he spread rumors that Raisa was HIV

Dr. Yakov Gluzman.
(Photo courtesy of
Cold Spring Harbor
Laboratories/Jane Reader)

Rita Gluzman.
(Photo courtesy Rockland
County, N.Y., District
Attorney)

Yakov and Rita Gluzman with their son Ilan at his
graduation from Drew University in 1991.
(*Photo courtesy U.S. Attorney's Office*)

The Gluzman home in Upper Saddle River, New Jersey.
(*Photo courtesy Tim Costello*)

Vladimir Zelenin was caught by police as he dumped Yakov Gluzman's body into the Passaic River from ECI Technologies' rear parking lot.   (*Photo courtesy Tim Costello*)

Yakov Gluzman was murdered as he entered his apartment in Pearl River, New York.   (*Photo courtesy Tim Costello*)

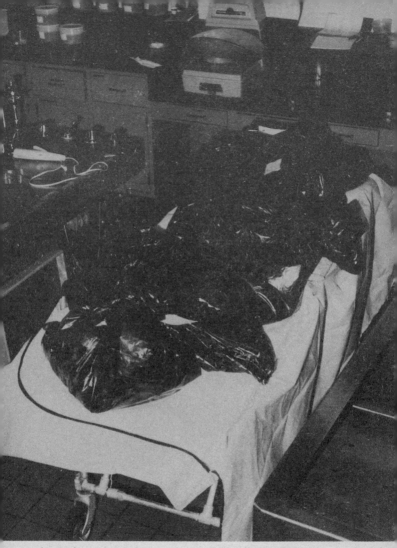

The eight garbage bags containing the dismembered body of the murdered man. (*Photo courtesy of Rockland County, N.Y., District Attorney and Bergen County, N.J., Coroner*)

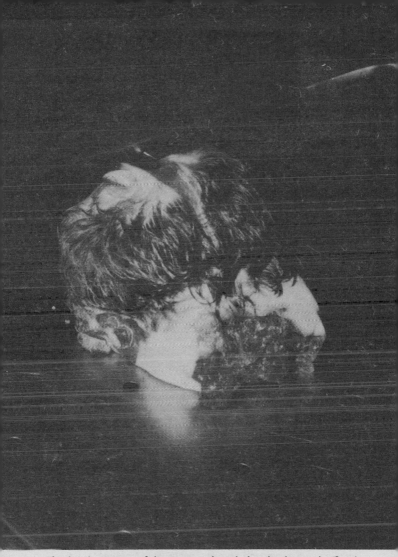

The back section of the victim's head clearly shows the fatal axe wound. *(Photo courtesy of Rockland County, N.Y., District Attorney and Bergen County, N.J., Coroner)*

The victim's fingertips were cut off his severed hands to prevent identification if they were ever recovered from the Passaic River. (*Photo courtesy Rockland County, N.Y., District Attorney* and *Bergen County, N.J., Coroner*)

The police found the still bloody knives, axes, hacksaw, hammer, garbage bags, and plastic gloves in Zelenin's car. (*Photo courtesy Rockland County, N.Y., District Attorney*)

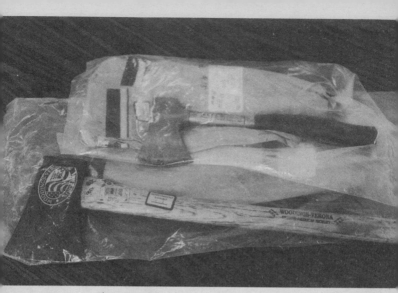

The axes which struck the killing blows.
(*Photo courtesy U.S. Attorney's Office*)

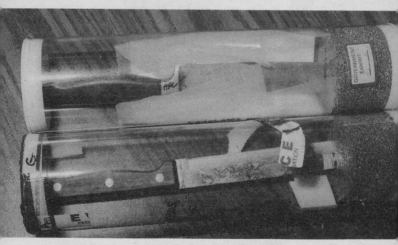

Rita Gluzman's preference for Henckel knives helped
tie her to the murder.
(*Photo courtesy Rockland County, N.Y., District Attorney*)

The bathroom where the victim's body was dissected by
his killers and put into plastic garbage bags.
(Photo courtesy Rockland county, N.Y., B.C.I.)

Lederle Laboratories in Pearl River, N.Y., where Yakov
Gluzman worked. *(Photo courtesy Tim Costello)*

Rockland County Deputy Sheriff/Criminal Investigator Jake Szpicek (*far left*), F.B.I. Special Agent Hilda Kogut (*second from left*), Detective Steven Colantonio of the Rockland District Attorney's Office (*center*), and Michael Gluzman, the victim's brother (*far right*) with three members of the Hadera Police Department in Israel. (*Photo courtesy Jake Szpicek*)

Rockland County, N.Y., District Attorney Michael E. Bongiorno. (*Photo courtesy Tim Costello*)

(*Left to right*) Assistant U.S. Attorney Cathy Seibel, Special Assistant U.S. Attorney Lou Valvo, and Assistant U.S. Attorney Deirdre M. Daly. (*Photo courtesy Tim Costello*)

Defense attorney Michael Rosen. (*Photo courtesy Tim Costello*)

Vladimir Zelenin at his arraignment for the murder of Yakov Gluzman. (*Photo courtesy Peter Monsees, The Record, Hackensack, N.J.*)

Rita Gluzman following her arrest in Cold Spring Harbor, N.Y. (*Photo courtesy Terrence James, The Record, Hackensack, N.J.*)

POLICE

positive. When the private investigator didn't go along with the suggestions, and when her wiretapping and her extortionate threats didn't do anything to stop Yakov Gluzman's resolve to divorce, the defendant's thoughts turned to murder.

"And to whom did she turn to assist her in the murder? Her cousin, Vladimir Zelenin, the one individual in the world who was almost competely dependent on her. Zelenin, you will learn, was a widower, with two children, new to the United States, not authorized to work here, speaking little English. The defendant was good to Zelenin, giving him a job at ECI and an ECI company car, and letting him and his children stay in the apartment in Fair Lawn that ECI paid for."

Seibel told the jury of Zelenin's cooperation, first with Rita, then with the prosecutors. She recited the details of the crime. Of the stop at CVS to buy bandages. Of Rita's flight, and her discovery five days later at Cold Spring Harbor. Then Seibel outlined the five counts with which Rita Gluzman was charged. Finally she interjected Vladimir Zelenin's plea agreement with the government: the accomplice would receive a minimum of twenty years behind bars for his role, regardless of the outcome of Rita's trial. She regretted too that the confessed killer was their best witness, but told the jury of his significance to them.

"Ladies and gentlemen, you're not going to like Vladimir Zelenin," Seibel said sternly to the jurors. "And rightfully so. He did an unspeakable thing and his reasons for doing so don't remotely begin to justify his actions. But the question of whether Vladimir Zelenin did something terrible is not at issue in this trial. Everyone is going to agree that he did it, including Zelenin himself."

Then the prosecutor got to her major point, which

she'd spent months establishing: "The issue is whether Vladimir Zelenin is telling the truth when he tells you about Rita Gluzman's participation in the murder. It will be up to you to evaluate his testimony, to decide if he has more to gain by lying or by telling the truth and you'll decide if the other evidence corroborates or supports his testimony."

Seibel then elucidated the corroborating evidence— months of accumulated physical evidence found by the detectives, other witnesses—502 pieces of evidence collected by Tom Goldrick, Tom Hoffmann, and Steve Colantonio together with sixty-eight pieces of Yakov Gluzman's body, the videotape of David Rom, and the murder weapons: the axes, the hatchet, and the Henckel knives.

As a precaution, Seibel added that there would be no great display of DNA charts, hairs, and blood to drag them astray from the core of the prosecution's case: that Rita Gluzman had conspired with her cousin to kill her husband. Then, as professionally as she'd begun twenty-five minutes before, Cathy Seibel ended her opening statement by informing the jurors, "If you keep an open mind, and examine the evidence, the government submits that the defendant will get a fair trial and the government will get a fair trial—and you will find the defendant guilty as charged."

It was a flawless opening, uninterrupted by any second thoughts on the part of the prosecutor. Seibel had prepared well, and her opening was delivered without a hint of sanctimony. Getting the jury to accept her months of work was now the task awaiting her.

When it was Larry Hochheiser's turn to open, the veteran defender rose and confronted the jurors, who had struck the lawyer as having been absorbed by Seibel's statement.

"Your Honor, ladies and gentlemen of the jury, let me start by saying that Rita Gluzman is absolutely innocent and the evidence will show that," Hochheiser said. "And those should be my first words and my last words. It's very difficult to stand here with the responsibility of a woman's fate in my hands. I feel in a sense like an athlete who wonders whether he has a good day or a bad day because this is an adversary system."

Explicating the win-lose system of criminal jury trials, Hochheiser complimented Seibel offhandedly as he complained of the government's "purity" by virtue of its position. He had argued in too many criminal trials to let the government get the upper hand early, and Hochheiser was fond of his Matlock-style manner in communicating with the jurors.

"Now, it's pretty awesome to hear an opening statement with allegations such as Miss Seibel made, and I can tell you that it's chilling and frightening for a lawyer with my responsibility to sit here and listen—and now I understand why Judge Parker tells you in the beginning to be careful to remember that this is not evidence. Would you feel as impressed if what was told you about how this murder was committed and what Vladimir Zelenin did and what Rita Gluzman is said to have done, would you feel as impressed if instead of being told by Cathy Seibel, a representative of the United States government, if Vladimir Zelenin stood here and told you that? The answer is no, you would be very skeptical. You're not skeptical of Cathy Seibel because she carries the mantle of the United States government. You would be damn skeptical if Vladimir Zelenin stood here and told you that!

"Vladimir Zelenin did stand here and tell you that because Cathy Seibel doesn't know anything more than what they decided they were going to accept from Vladimir Zelenin." Noting that Zelenin's story had changed from its initial telling after his arrest, Hochheiser suggested that it had been carefully crafted by the prosecutors to make a case against Rita Gluzman where none existed. The lawyer then tried to deconstruct the evidence against his client, noting the absence of hair and blood evidence, but drew mainly upon his own experience as a skeptic.

"You may look at me and be saying, why should we listen to him? Sure, this guy, he gets paid by Rita Gluzman. You're absolutely right. You shouldn't be listening to me even if I am telling you the truth and His Honor told you that. She would swear it's this way, and I'd swear it's the other way, and she gets paid by the United States Attorney and I get paid by the defendant, and that wouldn't work, would it? So I'm asking you to sit here and look at the evidence with us as it goes in and see what's really going on.

"When I say to you that I would look at me skeptically, I would also have to ask myself this question: Why am I so skeptical? Do I sit here and believe that innocent people do not go to trial? Do I sit here and believe that these three lawyers and these two FBI agents are so infallible that only guilty people come to trial? We wouldn't need jurors if that were true. We wouldn't have chosen you. So as you sit here and listen to me and listen to the evidence in the case, ask yourself: what does the trial of an innocent person look like? Now the trial of an innocent person looks in this courtroom, and all the courtrooms across America, very much like the trial of a guilty person. The difference is in that question of 'he said, she said'—says who? If Vladimir Zelenin were telling the truth, he would be corroborated, he would be verified.

"Vladimir Zelenin, to say that he is an animal is to

give a bad name to animals, because animals don't act that way. You cannot believe how he cut [Yakov] up and the government will tell you, you won't like Vladimir Zelenin well. Vladimir Zelenin is a witness who is in the position—this is just the way my mind works—in a manner similar to the movie *The Crucible*. It's about witchcraft, and it's an allegory for the McCarthy events, but it was about the witchcraft trials in the 1600s in Massachusetts. They told you they saw that gentleman, that lady with the devil. Today for witchcraft we substitute conspiracy. The witch, the coldblooded murderer, Vladimir Zelenin, comes in and says, 'I saw Rita Gluzman with the devil,' and the government takes this witness to their bosom. The government, these people who are the government, they accept what this guy says . . . this is the person who just gave you an opening statement through the lips of Cathy Seibel as to what happened here."

Hochheiser was energized. He had only wished that he and Rosen had been allowed to pick the jury of their choice, as he could at the state level. Dour, tall but not towering, with a baggy suit, the serious but folksy Hochheiser carried himself like a college professor, albeit with a few rough edges. Jury trials were his forte, and usually the shrewd attorney could convince a typical jury of at least some doubt of his client's absolute guilt. This jury would be tough, he knew at the outset, but his client's freedom was on the line, and Hochheiser continued his opening.

Rita Gluzman's attorney recited his client's life, beginning in the Ukraine, as though he were submitting a nomination to *Who's Who*, or possibly for a humanitarian award. Hochheiser soothed the jurors as he told of Rita's early hardships, then of her meeting and falling in love with Yakov, and of the tenacity and dedication to her

husband she'd displayed in winning his freedom from
the evil empire that had been the USSR. It was Rita who
had sustained the young family while Yakov earned his
Ph.D., Rita who nurtured Ilan and her husband, and
got them to America. It might as well have been Rita
who discovered the cancer cell at Cold Spring Harbor, as
far as Hochheiser's presentation went. Then he covered
ECI and Rita's drive in building it. Hochheiser
explained his affection for the justice system, and told
the jurors how he'd follow the rules in defending Rita,
but then he came to the most important point of his
opening, the businesslike meaning of the trial.

"You should try to understand," Hochheiser told all,
"why I don't undertake the burden to try to prove not
only this client but any client to be innocent because
His Honor is going to explain to you that is not what
the question is.

"The question is, did these people prove beyond a
reasonable doubt Rita Gluzman's guilt, not whether I
proved she is innocent. There are cases where sometimes a jury never knows what happened at the end.
There are cases where lawyers never know what happened at the end, but you do not know that an innocent
person is not going to be convicted if you follow those
rules, that you will acquit unless the government proves
the defendant guilty beyond a reasonable doubt. That's
what innocence means to us under these rules."

It was his standard guilt vs. innocence speech, but it
had often proved effective for Hochheiser. The lawyer
was fond of movie analogies, using lines from his favorites frequently. He recalled *In the Heat of the Night* for
the jury.

"It's chilling to me when a prosecutor stands up—

they all start with, 'This is a case about drugs and money and murder', you know, it's like a book. This is a case about murder, and whatever, and then comes the introductions. It's like a movie and then comes the titles and the actual story. But okay, that's salesmanship, but it chills me when I hear a prosecutor say it, without hearing the cross-examination, because the trial hasn't taken place, it's never taken place . . . Cathy Seibel is telling you in different words, 'I got a motive which is money and a body which is dead,' " the lawyer told the court, invoking Rod Steiger's memorable line. "Don't confuse me with facts. I got a motive which is money and a body which is dead. That's the government's position here. It doesn't stand up to logic."

Hochheiser proceeded to attack Seibel's argument that the divorce was hostile, that Yakov and Rita had financial disputes and had fought over control of ECI. The defense explained how hiring private investigators wasn't unusual in marriages, and how the couple had continued to have sex even when they'd been separated, and why the laundry list of items entered into the government's case as corroborative evidence wasn't proof of anything other than the natural human conflicts between two people and Rita's concern for her financial security during her divorce. It was an eloquent presentation.

Hochheiser kept returning to Zelenin, and reminded the jury that the star witness against his client—the only witness to have seen the crime—was a man so depraved that he chopped up the husband of his cousin and even shaved his victim's fingerprints off. Some jurors cringed inside themselves when the lawyer repeated the crime, and Zelenin's nonchalance in his choice of murder weapon.

The U.S. Attorney seemed not to have found a smoking gun in the case of U.S. v. Gluzman. No uninterested eyewitness, no blood or hair or other direct physical evidence that could prove conclusively that Rita Gluzman had been in the Pearl River apartment the night of April 6, 1996, with her cousin Zelenin as the Russian struck her husband with an ax, then dismembered him and disposed, or tried to dispose, of his victim Yakov Gluzman's body. Nothing, it seemed, but Vladimir Zelenin.

With natural cropped brown hair and a scholarly look, Cathy Seibel looked as tidy as the editor of the *Law Review* or maybe *The Economist*—academic yet down-to-earth—and cut a credible figure for the U.S. Attorney in the Quarropas courtroom. There was nothing pretentious or self-righteous about her. If she were telling people that Rita Gluzman had participated in the killing of her husband, what could they think about this prosecutor? Why else would she be saying these things about Rita Gluzman after working more than six months on the case if they weren't true? That was Hochheiser's dilemma. Seibel was attractive and businesslike, and hadn't spent more than $30 on her haircut, most likely gotten during her lunch hour while reviewing cases, and her wardrobe was presentable but neither expensive nor trendy, or beyond the reach of the working- and middle-class jurors. She and Daly struck observers as believing in the case against Rita without equivocation, and without ambition. When the trial was over, each would return to her work for another day. It was All-America versus the hired guns. Truth versus spin.

As Hochheiser began to deride the government's case, thirty minutes into his opening, Seibel raised her first objection after the defender had challenged the integrity of the witnesses and tapes. Judge Parker demurely but authoritatively informed Hochheiser that his opening statement was over, and that the trial was to begin. And that was that. To some in the room, Hochheiser seemed outmanned, and outgunned already, and the trial was only beginning.

Fourteen

Alternating with Cathy Seibel, Deirdre Daly called as her first witness Yakov's divorce lawyer, Nicholas Nasarenko, a matrimonial specialist the biologist had hired in May 1995 to put together a settlement agreement for Rita when he'd decided to divorce her. Establishing conflict between the Gluzmans from the outset was a reasonable strategy by the prosecutors, and Nasarenko, who had seen a number of divorces in twenty years as a lawyer in New Jersey, had been brought to the court to testify to Yakov's generosity toward Rita in the first offer he made. Nasarenko told the court how Rita had rejected the first offer because it enabled Yakov to keep stock in ECI, and Rita had wanted full control over the company. She'd also wanted the $300,000 loan on the company's books that represented Yakov's capital to be erased by paying her husband $100,000 and having him forgive the balance.

When Nasarenko explained New Jersey's "no-fault"

divorce law, the jury got an idea of what the Gluzmans faced: Yakov had left the Upper Saddle River house in early 1995, and after eighteen months of separation, either party could file for divorce and it would automatically be granted. Only the property settlement would need to be agreed on. Yakov was just several months away from being free from Rita. There was no cause for adultery under no-fault, making moot any claims by Rita that Yakov had carried on an affair with Raisa Korenblit, as she had done in her response to his divorce suit.

During the separation, Yakov had wanted to see ECI's records, his lawyer said; Yakov still owned fifty percent of ECI, but Rita refused during 1995 and 1996 to let her husband see the company's books and she had, in fact, threatened him with a restraining order preventing him from entering the office at One Madison if he had continued to try to inspect the operations of the business he'd financed.

Daly's intent was to show the disputes between the Gluzmans after Yakov had moved out and offered his wife a large sum, which she refused, to get the divorce speeded along. Rita presented continual obstacles to the settlement offer, especially when it challenged her authority to control ECI.

Hochheiser came out firing at Nasarenko, questioning the divorce lawyer's contention of the many disputes between Rita and Yakov. The defender seemed to attack the witness, and Judge Parker admonished Hochheiser privately to control his attacks on what was only the first witness in a trial expected to last more than a month. It was a harbinger of things to come: Larry Hochheiser trying to impeach the testimony of a prosecution witness. Ordinarily, the cumulative effect of such a strategy, over the several weeks of a trial, might be effective in wearing down the prosecution's witnesses and therefore its case, in front of the jury. Judge Parker was stunting the defense's efforts early on.

Hochheiser had already begun playing the reporters covering the trial, and Cathy Seibel confronted the defender about a comment he'd made on the eve of the trial, two days before, which was reported by the White Plains paper, something to the effect that Rita Gluzman's trial would be akin to the drama *The Crucible.* With an unsequestered jury able to read that day's paper, Seibel questioned Hochheiser's motives, suggesting the lawyer had set out to poison the jurors over the government's intent.

"I had the pleasure of reading in the paper yesterday," Seibel told Judge Parker, "about an allusion by Mr. Hochheiser to *The Crucible,* and it seems to me to run clearly afoul of the court's free press, fair trial directives that there will be no comments made about the credibility of the witnesses prior to the trial beginning. At the break this morning, there was a mini-press conference by Mr. Hochheiser in the courtroom, and while I know our jurors are not going to be reading the papers or watching the media—but that contact inadvertently comes to the attention of a juror. I would ask Your Honor to direct that those comments not be made, certainly not in the courtroom and not in the courthouse."

Hochheiser cut Seibel off. "First of all," he told Judge Parker, "we were here in the courtroom and there were no jurors walking by, and secondly, all the information that was in the article comes from the government. The only conversation I had was with an Associated Press reporter who wasn't asking me for opinions or facts. He was asking me 'How are you going to try this case? What are the issues in this case?'" Then he turned to Seibel. "You know, you go off half-cocked when you are dealing with someone's credibility. You don't seem to be too concerned. You did that with Benny Lefkowitz, which you're going to find out is not so—" Hochheiser stopped his thought. "You called me a liar and now you go before a federal judge—"

"Are you addressing me or the court?" Seibel asked the heated Hochheiser.

"I'm talking to you, lady. A couple of reporters asked me if I would be able to identify the relatives of my client, whether my client is going on the stand, et cetera, and none of these things were spoken about. There was nothing about the evidence, there was no opinion, there were no facts. [The reporters] asked what time is the break, what time is lunch. It was not a press conference. Some of these people wanted to know things from me, most of which I didn't want to tell them." Hochheiser was cooling off. Seibel was nonplussed.

It was Judge Parker's turn to address the press leak issue. "You're not following practice in this case of having substantive discussions with the press or trying this case outside the courtroom?" he asked Hochheiser.

"I am not."

"Well," Parker responded, dryly, "I think that goes a long way towards alleviating everybody's concerns." The judge had known in late December that this trial would be contentious. He tried with diplomacy to quell the discord between Hochheiser and Seibel as quickly as he could.

"In addition to a running a formal courtroom," the judge told Hochheiser at sidebar, "we run a civil courtroom, and I don't know what the evidence would show, but there were, I thought, some rather strong statements in your opening about the government's possible use of evidence that they knew to be incorrect or false, and I don't know what is there," the judge continued, "but statements like that are not made lightly and I'm certainly not likely to find they were made unnecessarily."

Hochheiser had let the judge know he meant business in Rita's defense, though, and asked Parker "What kind of thing is that to say to a lawyer trying a case? You're going to scare me to the point that I can't help my client!"

"You said we put on perjured testimony!" Daly told him.

"I said you held your nose when you took the testimony from an obvious liar, from Mike Rizzuto [the man who installed recorder in Gluzman's apartment]," Hochheiser said to Daly. "Anyone who reads the grand jury testimony knows he is a liar and anybody who listens to the CVS clerk knows that nobody cares, and they held their noses and they took their testimony. If you were on the other side, you would have—"

Parker interrupted them. "We're just getting started in this case. We run a civil operation here. I want to keep the tone of this whole proceeding where it should be and you all are a group of very accomplished professionals. I have no reason to expect any kind of conduct from anybody here that is not in accord with the highest standards, and we're not going to have that kind of animosity coming from anybody unless there is a really good reason for it."

Hochheiser's attempts to impeach the government's minor witnesses before their testimony had put Daly and Seibel on guard. They both had fairly good ideas what the two defense lawyers had in mind for Vladimir Zelenin, and if this was how they planned to cross-examine the supporting players such as Yakov's divorce lawyer, or Lenny Huffman from the CVS pharmacy, the prosecutors, with the judge as their mediator, had to act at the beginning to thwart Hochheiser and Rosen from browbeating everyone.

And the *Crucible* comment had struck a sensitive chord with the prosecutors. Arthur Miller's play about the McCarthy era and witnesses who testified as they believed the government wished them to was a disturbing analogy for Seibel and Daly, and an insult by Hochheiser to the federal prosecutors and detectives.

After lunch, Hochheiser resumed his questioning of Nasarenko, hammering over and over the details of Yakov's offer to Rita, and trying to negate the impact of the dispute over control of ECI on an eventual divorce. After an afternoon of questioning, it still appeared to the jury that Rita had been unrelenting, had wanted full control over the company her husband had funded with $300,000, and that an angry Rita hadn't even wanted to share the financial standing of the community asset with her husband even as he offered her the majority of the company's stock.

Fortunately for Rita Gluzman, she had hired as her attorney in the divorce action Barry Croland, one of the more respected matrimonial lawyers in New Jersey, who had communicated Rita's concerns during 1995 to Nasarenko, and had tried to keep a dignified appearance for his client while the minor maelstrom over ECI's control was being argued. But after all had been said and done, it was clear to the court that Yakov Gluzman had anted up to Rita nearly every liquid asset he had earned during their marriage, hundreds of thousands of dollars in cash, just to be free of her. And she had rejected his offer.

When it had become apparent to Yakov that his tender to Rita of the majority of the couple's assets in order to finalize a divorce with her wouldn't succeed,

Yakov had hired another lawyer, Jon Auty, in early 1996 to file the divorce action against Rita, which Auty, the next witness, testified was going to be strongly contested, owing to the disagreements between the two over money and ECI. This time Yakov, through Auty, sought equitable distribution of the couple's assets, a standard procedure in New Jersey family court. This meant, too, that Rita would probably get less than Yakov's prior offer if the divorce proceeded through superior court. Yakov had been fed up with the lack of progress in reaching an agreement with his wife of twenty-seven years, had tried to smooth the inevitable divorce along by offering all but some "start-over" capital to his wife, but she evidently wanted more, hence the filing for equitable distribution.

Deirdre Daly then got to the crux of the prosecution's use of the divorce lawyers on the stand. She asked Auty about the reasons Yakov had wanted to dissolve his marriage to Rita.

"On what grounds did Yakov Gluzman sue for divorce?" Daly asked.

"Extreme cruelty," Auty replied.

"Is that a standard ground for divorce in New Jersey?"

"New Jersey has a number of grounds and that was the one that I determined he was able to file under," Auty told them.

"Generally, what were the allegations filed in the divorce complaint?"

Hochheiser interrupted the prosecutor's examination of her witness, objecting stridently.

The lawyer tried vainly to exclude Auty's answer as to the reasons for Yakov's final actions: he had filed on grounds "for extreme mental cruelty," not an ordinary measure. Judge Parker overruled Hochheiser.

"Generally," Auty continued, "he was unhappy with the way—"

Hochheiser had had enough. "Excuse me! Your Honor, this is a whole area I would really like to discuss at sidebar."

Parker heard the lawyer's argument to exclude Auty's recollection of Yakov's feelings towards Rita.

"Your Honor, the government has placed into evidence from the prior witness a proposed property settlement and responses. These documents are factual, they're legal. They're proposals and counterproposals. What we're getting into now is documents which are venom. They have all kinds of negative characterizations. They make all kinds of accusations. They defame each other, call each other liars, et cetera.

"These documents are not documents that come in or should come in, I submit, wholesale, because they contain all this prejudicial heresay by both sides. And what's going to happen is, we're in the thicket of two people that the jury may never hear, calling each other all kinds of vile names and making all kinds of claims which can't be disputed or confirmed—we're going to litigate the divorce case! I mean, that's not what I'm anticipating he's being asked to do, but she can't ask him to say this."

Judge Parker intervened. "Where are we going?" he asked Daly.

"It was my intention to elicit testimony from the witness," Daly answered, "and then offer the statements of the defendant. Essentially, what occurred, there was a divorce complaint, and an answer. The defendant filed a petition for support. There was a response and a reply to that. I was going to offer all of those and elicit testimony . . . it's not hearsay. The reason I'm trying to get in what he filed as well is her papers are essentially reactive papers filed in response to what [Yakov] says and don't make any sense unless you know what he's filed."

"My objection was about hearsay and characterization," Hochheiser told Parker. "[The divorce filing] is a document that has facts in it and admissions by my client, but it also has hearsay claims and character assassinations and very negative characterizations like 'liar,' and things like this."

Daly shot back. "Your Honor, the fact that the divorce was an acrimonious divorce is relevant to this trial because there was an acrimonious divorce and this defendant had a financial motive to want her husband dead. That was our opening. That's going to be the proof in this case. The fact of what the divorce says is clearly relevant to show her state of mind."

Finally, Mike Rosen, who had been listening to the others for some time, decided to get his thoughts across to Parker. "Judge, if you allow something like this, whether it's [Auty's] testimony as to what he thinks is a viable cause of action, or these papers which claim personal cruelty, you're allowing Yakov Gluzman to testify from the grave and he can't be cross-examined."

Parker had heard from both sides. The judge agreed with Rosen's reasoning, and disallowed the "cruelty" statement, while keeping the door open for Deirdre Daly to continue questioning Jon Auty about the reasons for the couple's divorce.

"Mr. Auty," Daly resumed. "Without telling me exactly what those allegations were that were set forth in the divorce complaint, would you summarize for the jury generally the nature of the allegations?"

Again Hochheiser objected, and again Parker overruled him.

"It dealt mostly with financial issues," Auty replied.

"The issue was living beyond means, operating a business in such a fashion that he perceived problems."

"What, if anything, was discussed with respect to the corporation?" Daly asked, getting to the heart of the ECI dispute.

"He simply wanted to be apprised of the financial status [of ECI] and he felt he wasn't getting the information either from his wife or from the firm's accounting staff."

Yakov had had one option available to him to see ECI's books, a bit of leverage Auty had suggested his client could use to determine ECI's financial standing. Yakov could force a "deadlocked corporation," whereby ECI would be placed in temporary receivership until the shareholders—Yakov and Rita—reconciled their dispute. This had understandably upset Rita in early 1996, as she was about to be served with the divorce action. Then Rita had filed her claim for support from Yakov, listing expenses that even Manhattan's rich and famous would envy: vacation allowances, personal trainer and gym expenses, a hairdresser, and, as part of her normal monthly maintenance, a therapist. Rita had told Yakov, through her divorce lawyer Croland, that she'd need $11,000 a month to pay her bills, but was making only $50,000 a year from ECI. This only reaffirmed Yakov's determination to look at the company's books, as he realized his generosity toward his wife was being repaid with a steep invoice.

It became evident to observers that if Yakov Gluzman had possessed a fatal flaw, it was his trusting nature. Rita had been able to discover the existence of Raisa Korenblit, for example, only by intercepting a letter from Senator Bill Bradley to Yakov that had come to the Upper Saddle River home during their separation. New Jersey's senior U.S. Senator had written Yakov to inform the biologist (and constituent) that he'd been unable to help him obtain a visa for Korenblit to come to the U.S. The letter had been intended for Yakov alone, but had ended up in Rita's mail. Curious as to why Bradley would write her husband, she had opened the personal letter and been incensed at learning of Yakov's apparent desire to bring a woman she didn't know into the U.S. The jury hadn't been allowed by Judge Parker to hear the mental cruelty allegations, but they did hear about the girlfriend.

By the end of the first day of trial, the prosecutors had done a subtle but effective job of suggesting Rita Gluzman's "state of mind" in early 1996, not long before her husband ended up brutally murdered, much to the chagrin of Larry Hochheiser and Mike Rosen.

The trial's second day opened with one of the more entertaining witnesses, though a reluctant one, for the government's case. Joe Mullen was a longtime private investigator from New York City who had been recommended to Rita Gluzman by Barry Croland in the early stages of the separation and divorce action when Rita told her lawyer she suspected Yakov of adultery, before the issue of an affair had become a moot point. It had been Mullen's business card Carlos Rodriguez of BCI had found in the Gluzman garage's dryer duct.

Joe Mullen had spent more than forty years working as a detective and private investigator, mostly in matrimonial work, with time out to run a survival school with G. Gordon Liddy and some other retired agents in Florida. Mullen's wealthier clients sometimes used his services to check the backgrounds of people wishing to do business with them. The private investigator was a genuine New York character, a worthy description of a man whose life was engaged in the stuff of Mickey Spillane or Raymond Chandler novels, a classic detective in whose office one could envision clouds of smoke and a view of Times Square, a window of beveled glass with faint lettering on the outside indicating the visitor was entering a private eye's world.

Mullen was recuperating from a stroke he'd suffered in 1994, and explained to the court that he was afflicted with aphasia, a cruel neurological ailment stroke victims often developed following the catastrophic event. The aphasia would cause speech difficulties, with spoken words conflicting with intended statements. Daly made sure the jury understood the nature of Mullen's ailment, while reassuring them that his memory was unaffected.

Mullen remembered Rita Gluzman from her visit to his Manhattan office in September 1995. She had told Mullen that her husband was looting money from the family business and wanted the investigator to trace funds to Israel. She told him Yakov was sending the money from ECI to an Israeli mistress. She'd then shown Mullen the letter from Bill Bradley, and began deriding Raisa Korenblit. Mullen had suggested Rita find an investigator with ties to Israel, and brought up an associate, Bob Burton, who was a bounty hunter and a partner of G. Gordon Liddy in a Florida business. Mullen had charged Gluzman $1,000 for the consultation, declining additional work as he thought she would be best served by an overseas investigator.

Rita had seemed preoccupied with Raisa Korenblit to Mullen. Couldn't he help her keep Raisa from coming to the U.S.? Could he intervene with the Israeli police or the FBI to prevent Korenblit's leaving Israel? Rita had called Korenblit a prostitute, and repeatedly told Mullen the Israeli woman was a threat "to an American family," a phrase she used frequently during her afternoon-long meeting with Mullen. Rita was playing with the big boys now, and she seemed to know it.

Mike Rosen cross-examined Mullen, and tried to trip up the investigator's recollections. When did she come to visit you, exactly? Had his stroke affected his memory of certain events? Had he not referred her to a bounty hunter [Burton] with CIA ties? Remember this conversation, remember that? Rita's defender did his best to paint Mullen as a solicitor of an investigation into Yakov, not as a professional who had demurred after realizing Rita's obsessiveness.

Rosen's questioning continued: Had he seen the letter from Bill Bradley purportedly written to Rita? No, he'd taken Rita's claim at face value. Mullen referred to New Jersey's three-term U.S. Senator as "Congressman Bradley" and seemed to suggest that Mullen's own participation wouldn't be a crucial part of any investigation he might perform on Rita's behalf. After all, most of what she wanted required overseas help, and after supplying his new client with names of investigators in Israel and others whose contacts there might help her, Mullen had proceeded to recommend hiring an electronics man to do the sweep. Did he even know who Bill Bradley was? Rosen asked him.

"Yeah, is he getting a divorce?" asked Mullen, as some of the spectators chuckled for the first, perhaps the only, time in an otherwise severe criminal trial.

The prosecutors' next witnesses were the two men Joe Mullen had told Rita could perform an adequate job of detecting listening devices in her apartment—at least, Rita had told Mullen it was her apartment she wanted tested. Mike Rizzuto was in his thirties, an ex-con who testified he had decided to enter the surveillance business after serving time for a cocaine rap in the late 1980s, and had entered the growing "spy" business, with wiretapping equipment, micro-cassette recorders, and a swagger of the street. Rich people, Rizzuto found, had a need for his services. And they certainly looked the other way as the phone tapper went about his business.

Rizzuto told of meeting Rita Gluzman at the 7-11 in Pearl River not far from Yakov's apartment, and how she then had taken him and an associate of Mullen's to Celia Gardens, telling them she was afraid her apartment was being bugged, and asking if they would "sweep" the place to determine if there were any wiretaps. After Rizzuto had done a careful surveillance and told Gluzman there weren't any listening devices in the apartment, she had asked him to install one behind the refrigerator for her personal security. Though he thought it strange, Rizzuto agreed, and attached a tiny, business card-sized recorder to the phone jack behind the apartment's refrigerator. Rita had paid Rizzuto $750 by check, which he said covered the cost of the tape recorder and about a hundred dollars for his efforts. When asked why he had made so little on the transaction, and why he hadn't contacted Rita Gluzman afterward, Rizzuto told the court he just hadn't wanted to do further business with his strange customer. He and his associate had been somewhat intimidated by Rita.

It was Rizzuto's microcassette recorder the cops found in Zelenin's Taurus in East Rutherford. The prosecutors had now placed it in Rita Gluzman's hands months before Yakov's killing and showed Rita herself placing it in the Pearl River apartment to eavesdrop on her husband's conversations.

The sweeper was nervous. With a criminal record, no resources, and a terrific embarrassment resulting from his association with a client who may have killed her husband, Rizzuto was only too happy to cooperate with the prosecutors. They hadn't even made any money on the installation. Seibel and Daly realized the defense team would tear into both Rizzuto and his partner, Edwin Mateo, and dutifully had informed the defense and the judge of the criminal histories of the two witnesses prior to the trial as required under the Brennan law which disclosed "prior bad acts" of those called to the stand.

Deirdre Daly introduced her witnesses in careful order, so she and Seibel could prove the conspiracy and the extortion charges against Rita Gluzman. The U.S. Attorneys and Lou Valvo knew they'd need to establish a pattern in Rita's behavior, one which would demonstrate by her actions of 1995 into early 1996 a desperate need by her to save her marriage, to avoid "breaking up an American family," which would result in her tapping Yakov's phone, in harassing his girlfriend, Raisa (to the point of wanting her dead), and as Zelenin would testify, in injuring him to delay his travel to Israel (where he would reinforce his relationship with Raisa) until, finally, her desperation having reached a point of out-of-control rage, killing him.

Mike Rosen and Larry Hochheiser, at the defense table, knew they'd need to tarnish each of Daly's, Seibel's and Valvo's witnesses in order to poke holes in the government's case against Rita Gluzman. The trail she'd left, the "sweep" of Yakov's apartment, the hiring of the private investigators, the calls to David Rom in Israel, and, most crucial, her conversations with Zelenin, which he'd begun to record in March, didn't mean she had killed her husband. Rosen and Hochheiser suggested it was nothing more than ordinary self-protection when faced with a divorce action by a spouse with the greater financial power. By itself, Rita's inquiries to Mullen and Rom were essentially harmless, though indicative of a broken rapport between Yasha and Rita and her suspicion of his "other life." Her solicitation of the investigators to create an action, though, by causing harm to either Raisa or Yakov, warned the seasoned pros to back off from her, to avoid becoming accomplices to her unstated aims.

Michael Gluzman had flown in from Hadera, outside of Tel Aviv, to testify at his sister-in-law's trial. Yasha Gluzman's brother needed little preparation or encouragement. He was called with a Russian interpreter, as the younger Gluzman hadn't mastered English the way his brother had.

Michael Gluzman had followed Yakov to Israel in 1972, when he was eighteen, and had spent a lot of time with his brother and sister-in-law, until Yakov and Rita had moved to the U.S. The younger brother, a dentist, had remembered differences between the couple even in the early 1970s: Rita had told Yakov that his studies at Weizmann were not going to result in a successful career, and that maybe he should think of becoming a woodworker. Rita and Yakov quarrelled often, both in Israel and during the times Michael visited them in the U.S. It seemed to Michael Gluzman his brother and his wife were always fighting, more so than typical couples.

Hochheiser and Rosen both brought objections, sustained by Judge Parker, over the younger Gluzman's recollections of Yakov and Rita's relationship, claiming the prejudicial nature of a grieving and angry relative would unfairly prejudice the jury against their client.

Parker told Daly and the witness to restrict testimony to recent facts, events of Michael Gluzman's visits to see his brother in the 1990s. Yakov's brother then provided the shocker: Rita had told him, in 1991 or 1992, he said, in a private conversation in the kitchen at Upper Saddle River, that Yakov was no longer "good in bed." She seemed to be coming on to him. One night Yakov and Rita had taken Michael Gluzman and his wife for dinner in New York at Sammy's Rumanian, and Rita told Michael she would prefer to have a husband more like Michael than Yakov, this twenty-five years into her marriage to the older Gluzman.

Michael went on to tell the jury how he, his parents, and just about everyone else the family knew in Hadera was aware, in 1995, that Yakov was divorcing Rita, how his brother and Raisa Korenblit had spent a lot of time with the Gluzman family, and how it was laughable to suggest that Korenblit, a chemist, was a prostitute. Daly had asked Michael about the prostitution questions, raised in the extortion letter to Chaim Gluzman, his father, and by Rita to Joe Mullen.

Michael Gluzman said he wouldn't allow his brother to meet with a prostitute because the Gluzman family was so well-known in Israel. It was ludicrous that Korenblit, an agricultural biologist, would be thought of as a hooker. She could have made more money if she'd been a prostitute, Michael Gluzman said. Then he recited the contents of the first letter to Chaim Gluzman that he'd intercepted in October 1995.

"You, Dr. Gluzman [Yakov] have used the services of Raisa Korenblit and we ask you if you don't want your relationship with her to be published, to prepare $100,000, and taking into consideration that for such a rich person like you, there shouldn't be any problem getting such a sum. We will not submit these photo-

graphs to your wife, if you follow our instructions."
The photo in the extortion letter had been taken on
September 22, 1995, the note written in Russian, and
the amount, $100,000, was in keeping with the sum Rita
had alleged to her divorce lawyer that Yakov had sent
to his father in Israel. The second letter Michael Gluzman had received, in November 1995, reiterated that
Yakov was cavorting with a prostitute, and that for
$50,000, the letter writer would not send copies of the
photo of Yakov and Raisa to the major media outlets in
Israel. The writer had referred in the pasted-together
letters to Yakov by his familiar name, Yasha, a name that
only his close friends used. This had made Michael
Gluzman even more suspicious, and he had gone to the
Hadera police station to report the extortion plot. The
last letter had threatened Michael Gluzman's dental
practice, and had implied that for "protection" payments, his business would remain safe.

Michael Gluzman had been asked by the Hadera
police if the letter-writer might have been from organized crime. No, he told them; "If it's the mafia, I'm
from the moon." From the outset, he had suspected
Rita.

Suddenly, in early 1996, there were no further letters
and no follow-up to the letters written to Chaim Gluzman in late 1995. Yakov had visited Michael in Hadera,
in early January, the last time the brothers saw one
another. The time stuck in Michael's mind. The brother
was still grieving at the loss of Yasha, whom he had
looked up to, loved, respected for his accomplishments
in science, his success.

Raisa Korenblit was called to the stand next. Lou
Valvo did the direct examination, and asked Raisa about
her relationship with Yakov Gluzman. Yakov's acquain-
tance had travelled diligently to White Plains to testify.

Still in shock almost a year after Yasha's death, Korenblit nonetheless spoke firmly through her interpreter.

Raisa had met Yakov Gluzman in August 1994, at a shopping mall in Hadera. Trained as a physician in her native Moscow, Korenblit had emigrated to Israel in 1990, when she was twenty-nine, and found work as a food bacteriologist at a plant near Hadera. She had liked Yakov almost at once, and the two had begun a correspondence, and would see each other when Yakov visited Israel on business. Yakov would bring her small gifts, a Walkman, for example, with Julio Iglesias tapes, and, as 1995 proceeded, they became romantic. Yakov was her first boyfriend, at age thirty-four, Korenblit told the court. They had become intimate in September 1995. She testified that until that time, she had been a virgin.

Michael Gluzman had told Korenblit about the extortion letters, and she identified the photos and letter for Daly. She remembered the date the photos were taken, in September 1995, when she had worn the green chiffon dress that was in the photo. Korenblit then testified as to her own uneasiness in fall 1995, when she began getting phone calls late at night, from a male voice threatening her. After a week or so, in October 1995, a woman began calling her late at night, identifying herself as a representative of the Israeli Health Department. Speaking in hushed tones, she told Korenblit she had a chance to go to Netanya, north of Hadera, to work for the Ministry of Health. Someone will call you tomorrow, talk with him, the woman had told Korenblit. His name is Benny.

"Benny" showed up the next morning at Korenblit's flat in Akiva, the Hadera suburb where she lived. The man asked Korenblit about her relationship with Yakov Gluzman, strange for someone purportedly there to conduct a job interview. Raisa testified that it was only later that she had learned "Benny" was Benny Lefkowitz, the associate of David Rom, the private investigator Rita Gluzman had hired to check into Raisa's life. There was no job with the Health Ministry waiting for Korenblit.

Perhaps the most devastating comment that could come back to haunt Rita Gluzman was what she'd told each of the private investigators: Korenblit was "a cheap prostitute . . . an Israeli whore." No one else anywhere had ever chosen that term to describe the innocent-looking Korenblit, a shy young woman who worked in agriculture. Not only was she not a prostitute, those who knew her had laughed when asked if she had ever sold her services to anybody.

Only Rita Gluzman had ever called the quiet Korenblit a prostitute.

Bob Burton, the bounty hunter from Arizona, was a fairly renowned ex-CIA agent who had been partners with G. Gordon Liddy in a private detective school in Florida before relocating to Tombstone in 1991. The timing for this witness couldn't have been better: Burton had been the subject of a *60 Minutes* feature three days before his appearance at the White Plains courthouse. Burton had been a bounty hunter since 1959, with time off for a stint in the Marines and then as a CIA contract operative in South America in the late 1970s. Like Joe Mullen, Burton was another colorful hired hand Rita Gluzman had sought to prevent Raisa Korenblit from getting into the United States. But Rita had evidently become impatient with Yakov and Raisa Korenblit when she began calling Burton in early 1996.

Under oath Bob Burton told the jurors of Rita Gluzman's solicitation of him, how she'd called eight or nine times, using Mullen as a reference. Burton phrased Rita's request discreetly: she had wanted him to "intercede in the breakup in the marriage, perhaps inhibit the breakup, perhaps somehow take direct action which would inhibit the breakup," he told the court.

Rita had called the woman who threatened her marriage an "Israeli whore" Burton said. His putative client hadn't seemed love-lost either: Rita had had "no expressions of feelings in the sense of emotion, emotional caring . . . and it seemed distant from the personage of the husband . . . it was the abstract concept of the marriage that she wanted to keep intact." Burton had suggested Rita call an Israeli investigator he knew, Avram Siram. Rita had then asked Burton if he might plant cocaine on Raisa, or possibly transmit AIDS to the Israeli woman, perhaps putting the virus in a drink and serving it to Korenblit. It was at that point, in February 1996, that Bob Burton realized, he told Seibel, that he wasn't going to go further with Rita Gluzman as a potential client. His courtesy to Mullen fulfilled, Burton declined any payment from the woman, who had called him from an airport, telling the bounty hunter that she would fly to Arizona to see him.

Mike Rosen lit full-force into Burton on cross-examination, deriding the bounty hunter's appearance on *60 Minutes* as he recalled Burton's statements on the TV show that most of the time his job consisted of confronting stupid people. Then the defense lawyer tried to negate Burton's AIDS story: didn't he know that Rita Gluzman had a degree in chemistry, that she knew it was virtually impossible to infect someone with AIDS by passing the virus through a drink? But Burton's testimony had had its effect. The jury had heard more sworn testimony of Rita's obsession with Raisa Korenblit, of her attempting to hire worldly adventurers to deal with Yakov's new love interest, and to possibly do something violent to Korenblit.

Burton was excused following his cross-examination. The eight men and four women of the jury had heard an intriguing beginning to the tale of obsession, in which Rita Gluzman, it seemed, tried to do everything possible to save her marriage to a man whom she no longer appeared to love as much as she coveted, and to prevent his assignation with a younger woman six thousand miles away.

Daly called Yakov's next door neighbors from the Celia Gardens complex on Middletown Road, John Smith, a retired New York City police officer, and his wife Theresa. Their apartment was across the hall from the apartment Yakov had lived in. Mrs. Smitih testified that she had awakened early Sunday morning to the sound of a car alarm in the parking lot downstairs behind their apartment. Irritated by the noise at the crack of dawn, she looked out her window and saw two adults, a man and a woman, entering Yakov Gluzman's Nissan Maxima. The man was balding, and his companion wore a scarf and was distinctly feminine. She hadn't seen the woman's face. Mrs. Smith testified it was clear the couple were nervous about the car alarm, which they disengaged once the man started the engine.

The defense did not challenge the credibility of either Theresa or John Smith.

After the last person to see Yakov Gluzman alive Saturday night at Lederle was sworn in, the prosecution's timeline was fairly complete; Yasha's co-worker had left at the same time, 11:30 P.M. The woman had bade her friend and colleague goodbye. She hadn't realized at that moment it would be the last time she would see Yakov Gluzman alive.

Now, the main event was about to begin. Judge Parker ordered the marshals to bring Vladimir Zelenin into the courtroom, and the confessed killer of Yakov Gluzman was sworn for the start of the trial's most dramatic testimony.

Fifteen

Vladimir Zelenin had turned forty while sitting in the Rockland County jail awaiting his appearance at his cousin Rita's trial. His parents had rushed to the United States from Kyrgyzstan to watch over Igor and Gennade, Zelenin's two teenage sons. The confessed killer of Yakov Gluzman must have agonized since his arrest over the chain of events since he'd come to the U.S., and the way his life had turned out. Still, even looking at a minimum of twenty years away in a penitentiary, Zelenin might have thought it no worse than life in Kyrgyzstan, without the prison cell.

Zelenin would start Thursday afternoon, then resume the following Monday, as Judge Parker had established the court would be off Fridays so that he could conclude other cases before him. This would allow the defense three days to prepare its first cross-examination of the one prosecution witness who could most damage their client irreparably. The prosecutors, Lou Valvo, Cathy

Seibel, and Deirdre Daly, would warm up their chief witness the first afternoon, hoping he would tell the jury a few things about the plans leading to Yakov Gluzman's killing, then return Monday for the meat of his testimony.

Zelenin was first asked about his agreement with the government, what incentive the man had to testify in court as a cooperating witness, and he recited the terms: "I acknowledged my guilt in the state court that I had committed the crime together with Rita Gluzman. I acknowledged the killing in the second degree, and [in federal court] I have acknowledged the guilt I had, in order to commit the crime together with Rita Gluzman, crossed the borderline."

Then he added, "And I made the killing of Yakov Gluzman."

Zelenin told the court he was unaware what sentence he would receive for his testimony, how much the life sentence normally mandated for his confessed crime would be reduced owing to his cooperation with the government. Larry Hochheiser and Mike Rosen had challenged what the two defenders portrayed as a "deal with the devil," the confessed killer's arrangement with the prosecutors in order to give up their client. Would he serve ten years? Twenty? Or, like Sammy "the Bull" Gravano, would Vladimir Zelenin walk out the door after the trial a free man if his words were successful in convicting Rita Gluzman?

Zelenin explained that he had no idea how long he would be away, only that the U.S. Attorney told him he'd get a mandatory twenty years, no less, even if he helped them convict Rita. No less than twenty, he told them. It would be Judge Parker who would file the recommendation after he'd heard the witness's testimony and determined its value to the case. The attorneys argued the benefits: Hochheiser said that the jury might try to watch the judge's reaction more than observe the testimony itself, prejudicing them unfairly, Rita's lawyer explained. But Seibel seemed to defuse the defender's contention by noting that if it appeared Zelenin was lying, Parker would be the first to notice, and the judge might possibly move for no reduction in Zelenin's sentence. They would have to rely on the record, and on Parker's perceptions.

Then they heard testimony as to why he was there: "[The murder] occurred in the apartment of Yakov Gluzman ... in the state of New York, in Pearl River ... We crossed the state line of New Jersey, New York. We used axes. We both attacked Yakov Gluzman when he returned home, and after he died, his body was cut up, by me. I was cutting the body, and Rita Gluzman was cleaning the blood that was on the floor."

Seibel wanted Zelenin to detail his background, to perhaps tell the jury how he had gotten to be so desperate, how he had been lured into doing the unspeakable.

"I received my higher education in the Soviet Union," Zelenin told the court. "I studied six years in the Kyrgyzstan State University, in physics. When I finished the university, I had two degrees, one in physics metallurgy, the second in education. Then I worked at a factory in the capacity of an engineer. After that I worked as a teacher in high school, I taught physics, astronomy and trade school capacity. I had problems with the school administration, and that's why I was transferred to the trade school division. I had problems with anti-Semitism, and I had problems because at one time, I was like chairman of the union.

"In Kyrgyzstan, the majority of the population are Kyrgyz, Muslims. Then you have the Russians. Basically, they were Russian-speaking people.

"Among the Russian speaking, you had the Christians. The majority [though] in Kyrgyzstan were Muslims. Some Jews," he continued, "but the Jewish community is a very small percentage. My nationality is Jewish. [The] Russians will never say that they are Jewish, because in my country they were always persecuted."

After a fifteen-minute talk about how hard his life had been, and why historically the Jews were in such bad favor in his native Kyrgyzstan, Judge Parker interrupted Zelenin and Cathy Seibel. "Where are we going with all these current events?" the judge wondered.

"Two places with it, Your Honor," Seibel responded. "The witness is going to testify how petrified he was at the thought of going back to the Soviet Union. Second, the immigration application which the witness filed, which admittedly contains a number of falsehoods, also contains a germ of truth." Seibel went on to describe Zelenin's "political asylum" contention, and explain the witness' stretching of the truth in his immigration paperwork. Getting into the record, at the first opportunity, each of Zelenin's "prior bad acts" would quiet objections from the defense, which had prepared a lengthy dossier on Rita's cousin. They would attack his credibility at any chance.

"Okay, well let's move on," Parker said. It was clear the judge was a man who didn't enjoy seeing much time wasted by anybody in his courtroom, and he wasn't playing favorites with either the prosecutors or defense lawyers.

"After the Soviet Union fell apart," Zelenin continued through his interpreter, "in Kyrgyzstan, there were great changes and the nationality and the population began to change because the majority of the population were Muslims, and they turned out to be in such a way that Russian-speaking people began to flee. And those

people who had to reflect on the Jewish community,
they began to experience this growing Islam fundamen-
talism.

"I wanted to enroll in the medical institute, to study,
but they didn't accept my documents because of the so-
called 'fifth line,' " which was, Zelenin told them, "the
fifth line on any document in the Soviet Union is for
nationality."

There had been an incident, in 1991, that brought
it home. Zelenin was attacked in his apartment in Kygyz-
stan. He said they were nationalists, Islamic fundamen-
talists, that broke in and beat him up.

"I was working in the school, and I was the chairman
of the union. They would call me 'kike,' and we were
used to it. What they were saying was, 'you are a dirty
Jew and you have to be killed.' The Kyrgyz, they attacked
my wife, it turned out that I lost my consciousness. When
I had tried to intervene, one of them hit me over the
head. I have here a scar in my forehead. They thought
they had killed me."

It was a heart-rending tale, but not as overtly violent
on a continual basis to demonstrate a system of persecu-
tion of either Zelenin or all Jews in Kyrgyzstan, at least
not yet. Ten miles north of the Bronx, most of the jury
had heard far worse stories.

Zelenin told them he had been beaten up again in
1993, and it was then he realized it was time to move
away from his homeland. He caught a flight to the U.S.
It was in 1993 that Zelenin first stayed with his cousin,
Gregory Kogan, in Brooklyn. Kogan had helped Zelenin
fill out his immigration application, which they filed
in Chicago, due to the easier processing found in the
midwestern city. Zelenin testified Kogan would later
threaten to turn him in to the Immigration and Natural-

ization Service for lying on his application over the reasons for his seeking political asylum.

While staying in Brooklyn with Kogan, Zelenin met another cousin, Rita Gluzman. Then he learned that his wife had been killed back in Kyrgyzstan. It was an upsetting time, and Zelenin returned to Russia for his sons. Rita had then gotten Zelenin a tourist visa in order to return with the boys to the U.S. She also paid for his immigration lawyer in Chicago. A year later, in the summer of 1995, Rita hired Zelenin to do odd jobs at ECI. Rita had taken care of a number of family members, including her mother and sister, by hiring them to work at ECI. Also that summer, Rita got Zelenin the apartment in Fair Lawn, New Jersey, which her mother had used up until then. Then she provided a company car, the older Ford Taurus. Zelenin had gotten a social security number and a green card, thanks again to Rita.

After all this good fortune, Zelenin testified, Gregory Kogan had tried to blackmail him after he left Kogan's Brooklyn apartment. His cousin, Kogan, wanted $3,000. Zelenin, terrified that Kogan woud write INS about the dishonest immigration form, had given Kogan about $2,500 to keep him from turning him in. Zelenin had had only $200 at the time, but he'd found a way to come up with the additional money. Yakov Gluzman, Rita's husband, in the midst of the couple's separation, had loaned Zelenin $2,000 solely on the man's good word. Over the next few months, Zelenin had tried his best to repay the generosity of Yasha Gluzman, and had returned almost $1,900.

Gregory Kogan continued to bother him, Zelenin told the court. He wanted even more money and a green card. Zelenin was petrified.

Fortunately, Rita Gluzman had befriended Zelenin toward the end of summer 1995. Zelenin confided in her Kogan's threat without mentioning his demand for money and Rita assured her cousin that she would talk with their Brooklyn cousin, and try to quell his harassment. Then Rita confided in Vladimir a story of her own. She and Yakov had been separated almost all of 1995, and Yakov had found a lover, a woman in Israel, Rita told him. Rita also told Zelenin that her psychologist had advised her to do everything possible to keep Yakov. Over Larry Hochheiser's objection, Judge Parker allowed Zelenin to tell the court of Rita's purported discussions with a doctor that she had in turn relayed to him.

"Rita said that due to this problem [the girlfriend] she goes to see a psychologist, and this psychologist suggested that, at all costs, she should try to retain Yakov. And Rita used to say Yakov has to fly to Israel and there he is going to see this woman. And the psychologist said that you have to try at all costs to interrupt this. And then Rita said that something should be done so that Yakov will not be able to fly to Israel.

"It will not be bad if he will be beaten up or to make an automobile accident, so that he will be in no condition to fly to Israel. And she asked me if I could find some people who will be able to do it."

It was an astonishing comment, and Zelenin told the court that he had refused politely to help Rita hinder Yakov in the physical manner she had suggested. Zelenin had looked for a compromise, though, and had told Rita that perhaps she should feed her husband something that would have given Yakov strong diarrhea, and that that would prevent him from traveling.

Rita, in her frequent conversations with Zelenin, had told her cousin some details about the ongoing divorce battle she and Yakov were involved in. If it were to go through, Rita told Zelenin, Yakov would take control of ECI and he would lose his job and apartment.

Rita had another favor to ask of Vladimir Zelenin late in 1995: would he give her the phone calling card from the Fair Lawn apartment? She needed it for some personal calls she didn't want to appear on the ECI bill, or at Upper Saddle River. Zelenin had gladly given his cousin the MCI card from the Fair Lawn apartment, which was still in the name of Rita's mother, Paula Shapiro. It hadn't seemed like such a big deal. But when Seibel introduced the MCI bills related to the Shapiro calling card, the calls to Tombstone, Arizona appeared.

In February 1996 Igor Zelenin, Vladimir's sixteen-year-old son, broke his leg. The Zelenins were uninsured, and the new money problem had worried Vladimir. The medical bills mounted while he looked for a way to pay them, Zelenin told them.

In February 1996, Rita asked Zelenin to take a walk with her outside the ECI offices at One Madison, and when they did, Rita informed Zelenin that she had learned from Yakov of Gregory Kogan's shakedown attempt and of Yakov's loan to Zelenin, which she considered unwise. She reiterated her fear to her cousin that she would lose ECI and that they would all be out of work. For the first time, Rita had told Vladimir Zelenin that 'Yakov should be killed.' "

"I didn't try to talk her out of it," Zelenin testified. "I felt completely indebted to her, and I couldn't argue on anything with her." But he then realized how Rita had found out about his arrangement with Gregory Kogan. It hadn't been a direct conversation with Yakov; she had overheard it on a tape recorder she planted in Yakov's apartment in Pearl River.

What would he do if he lost his job at ECI, Rita had asked him repeatedly during February and into March.

"What are you going to do, where are you going to find a job, what are you going to do with your children?" Zelenin was haunted by his cousin's questions, but thought he had few options open to him other than cooperating with her in any fashion.

The day was ending, and Cathy Seibel had, she thought, done fairly well in outlining the conspiracy charge. Zelenin, who was being accepted by both Parker and the jury, was accounting for his time with Rita Gluzman, her suggestions to him, her anxiety over possibly losing ECI. There would be three days to review for both sides.

Sixteen

The two interpreters again reported for duty at Quarropas Street the morning of Monday, January 13, the second week of Rita Gluzman's trial. Natalia Kavaliauskas and George Markov, the two Russian émigrés who had found successful white-collar careers in the U.S. translating testimony for various courts throughout the New York area, settled down for another day of work, as did the prosecutors, their law enforcement gallery, Rita Gluzman's mother and sister Zelenin's sons and the witness's parents; and nearly a hundred press spectators and others. They all had waited anxiously over the long weekend to hear the next chapter in Vladimir Zelenin's saga. It wasn't often one had a chance to hear firsthand how one man had calmly bludgeoned and then dissected another person.

Zelenin told the jury how he and his cousin Rita went to Yakov's apartment for the first time in March 1996, and how it was during this first trip, during the day while Yakov was at Lederle, that he had learned of the tape recorder behind the refrigerator. Rita removed it then, and showed Zelenin the taping system. On the ride back to ECI that day, Zelenin had realized in his heart that he would go along with any plan Rita had to kill Yakov. She had asked him if he had access to either a gun or an ax. He was deluded and desperate. With nowhere else to live or work, and with Gregory Kogan bearing down on him for more money to stay quiet, Zelenin told the court, "I couldn't decline, because if I declined, then I would be thinking Rita will do everything possible in order to get rid of me and say return to Brooklyn or somewhere. I didn't have the means to do that. I had a lot of problems with Gregory Kogan . . . he promised to deport me. I was worried what will happen to my children.

"In one of the days after Rita came over to my place after work and we went to Home Depot," Zelenin continued. "And we bought the ax, and the hacksaw . . . the ax we were going to use in order to attack Yakov and kill him. The reason for the hacksaw was so that Yakov's body would be cut up. There was a conversation [with Rita] that Yakov is such a large man and that there was a problem how to get rid of the body, because in order to get the body out of the apartment, well, someone would notice it. That's why we decide that the body is going to be cut up.

"For all these items, Rita paid," Zelenin continued, after identifying the murder weapon Seibel showed him as the ax he and Rita had purchased at Home Depot.

They had discussed when to kill Yakov, Zelenin said. It was mid-March when they laid the groundwork. The divorce action was proceeding after Yakov's filing with Jon Auty, and time was of the essence. If Yakov were to die or disappear, Rita would receive the marital estate, all of it, excepting whatever Yakov had designated to go to Ilan. If the divorce proceeded as planned, she would get little, and she would lose ECI. They had about two weeks, Rita explained in the ride to Home Depot. Two weeks to kill Yakov, and to keep ECI from forced receivership.

After Rita had shown him the tiny tape recorder behind Yakov's refrigerator, Zelenin had gotten an idea. He decided to record his conversations with Rita. His cousin, while his only source of support, was possibly the kind of person who would betray him, Zelenin thought, and possibly abandon him after they had killed Yakov. Rita might feed him to the wolves, he theorized.

It was possibly the first time in several years that the Russian had had an undeniable suspicion, and luckily for him, he had acted on his idea. Shortly after, Zelenin began calling Rita on the telephone, just discussing casual things, small talk, and then asking more about the murder plans. Unbeknownst to Rita, he had hooked up an old tape recorder to the phone in his Fair Lawn apartment to keep a record of their conversations. On the tape, which the FBI had secured and transcribed, Rita and Vladimir talked about Yakov's routine on Saturdays. "He gets up late," Rita said, and then she described her husband's typical Saturday. "We should go in the afternoon, wait for evening," Rita continued.

It wasn't a "smoking gun," but it alluded to Rita and Vladimir Zelenin reviewing Yakov Gluzman's weekend in a manner that didn't suggest the two were planning a surprise birthday party for him, either.

On their second visit together to Yakov's apartment, Rita had noticed a box of prophylactics on her husband's bedside table. She told Zelenin, " 'Like father, like son'," the witness said. " 'He's just changing from

woman to woman'." She was mad at him, but not sorry
for him.

On the second visit, Rita and Zelenin had decided to
try their plan the next Saturday, the end of the month.
Their tools were ready, and they knew Yakov's schedule.
They would enter the Celia Gardens apartment, lay in
wait until Yakov returned from Lederle, just five minutes
down the street, and then kill him.

"We discussed that when Yakov was gonna come in
we're gonna attack him and I will use the big ax and
the knife and Rita is going to use the little ax and the
hammer.

"On March the 29th we waited [in the apartment]
for a long time," Zelenin told them, describing the
aborted first try by Rita and him to kill Yakov. "But
Yakov wasn't there. Rita said that Yakov always returns
home, so why don't we wait some more. Then we left."

Late Saturday, after Yakov had failed to show, they
gathered the weapons and drove off, down the road to
New Jersey.

The following Saturday was important as a deadline,
Rita told Zelenin. Yakov was scheduled to come to
Upper Saddle River sometime that weekend to get the
remaining things he had left at the family home since
their separation. Once he'd fully moved out, there
would be no reason for him to return to Upper Saddle
River, and Rita feared all would be lost, Zelenin said.
They would return to Pearl River the next weekend, on
Saturday, April 6th, she told her cousin. But first, it was
nearing Passover, and Rita had a family Seder planned
for the Upper Saddle River house. The following week,
on April 4, two days before their planned ambush, Rita
had gathered the Shapiro clan at her home for the start
of Pesach, a holiday whose traditional meaning lent
irony to the cousins' current plan of murder. Zelenin,

drank Manischewitz with matzoh ball soup and enjoyed the Seder. The spectre of death for Yakov was two days from arriving.

Saturday, April 6, Zelenin continued, they would go to Pearl River, in Zelenin's Taurus, and park behind the complex. At Rita's house in Upper Saddle River, before they departed for the thirty-minute ride north, Zelenin told them, "I [had a] smoke, then Rita was doing something within the house. I took all the tools and all the bags, all the plastic bags and the paper bags [that they would use to carry out the body]. And I put everything into my car. I placed the bag where was found the ax, also in this bag was placed the knife, also the hammer was placed inside, the flashlight, and the hacksaw was there.

"This knife was taken from the kitchen, from that set of knives," Zelenin continued. The set of Rita Gluzman's Henckel knives, Cathy Seibel pointed out. Rita had a glimmering set of the expensive knives on the sink of her kitchen at Upper Saddle River.

The hammer Zelenin described was from Rita's garage. It would be useful in attacking Yakov. They had bought the garbage bags at the local Grand Union supermarket. Zelenin took a pair of Rita's pantyhose to use as a mask in the event he needed one at Pearl River.

"On that day we stopped at the 7-11. Rita called [Yakov's apartment] and it turned out Yakov wasn't home and we went and we stopped on the parking lot next to his house. After we stopped there, we went into Yakov's apartment."

Cathy Seibel's direct examination of her star witness was proving successful. There weren't too many objections brought by either Larry Hochheiser or Mike Rosen, owing to both the venue of federal court, where more gentlemanly rules of conduct prevailed, and to their strict attention to Zelenin's statements, which they would need to challenge on cross-examination. The use of an interpreter was slowing the process somewhat. The prosecutors were happy, though; the slower tone worked in their favor.

He and Rita had entered Yakov's apartment late Saturday afternoon after their phone call from the 7-11, and waited for hours before they noticed his car drive up in front of the complex. Neither had displayed to the other any second thoughts about the evil they were about to do.

Positioning himself at the front door, Zelenin stood so that he would be at the left side of anyone entering the apartment. Rita Gluzman stood in the doorway, facing the front. Zelenin was holding the axe and a knife. Rita had the other ax and the hammer. Yakov had parked his Nissan Maxima in the Celia Gardens tenants' lot, away from the lot where Zelenin's Taurus was parked. He walked up the eighteen steps to the second-floor landing, and turned right to open his door. It was just before midnight. The biologist opened his apartment door, and was greeted with a blow from Zelenin's ax, across the forehead at the front of his scalp. At that moment, Yakov Gluzman's life came to an end. Rita also had struck at her husband, hitting both Yakov and Zelenin, and the confluence of both axes had killed Yakov. Zelenin had struck again, but he and Rita realized that their initial blows had done the job. Yakov fell to the floor, Zelenin dropped his ax and knife and ran to the bathroom to wash the wounds on his hand from Rita's weapon.

Zelenin described the apartment in the aftermath of the brutal but quick murder he and Rita had just committed. "I came out of the bathroom, and I saw that Rita was trying to push rags on some sort of runway to cover Yakov because there was bleeding. I moved Yakov's body into the bathroom, into the bathtub, and I went out of the apartment for a smoke.

"When I came back into the apartment I couldn't do anything because my fingers were wounded quite deeply. I said to Rita, 'I have to wrap it up somehow,' and we decided that we would go to her house, we're gonna wrap the hand and then return."

Taking the Taurus back to New Jersey, Rita and Zelenin left Yakov's body in the bathtub of the apartment, and after midnight headed to Upper Saddle River. They got to Rita's home and she saw Ilan's car in the driveway. Rita ascertained Ilan wasn't home, and the two killers entered the house to clean up. Rita had blood on her pants. She changed her clothing and washed the pants in the washer with a good deal of Clorox, Zelenin told them, as that would get all the blood out. The two drove back to Yakov's apartment, arriving there at 2 A.M. Daylight Savings Time was beginning, and they were going to lose an hour. Donning gloves, they began cleaning the entryway inside Yakov's apartment, and while Rita cleaned the hallway, Zelenin started to cut up Yakov Gluzman's body. The cold, dead corpse had stiffened while laying in the bathtub during the two-hour absence of his killers.

How did he know what to do, asked Cathy Seibel. Did you have any experience with cutting up bodies?

"I didn't have any experience ever about how to cut a body," Zelenin explained. "But I did—I used to take animals apart where I lived. It was natural. Everybody knew how to cut up an animal. Also, I did hunting, so I knew how to cut up an animal." He had used "the knife, the hacksaw, and the hammer."

What had happened while he was carving, asked Seibel.

"I broke the knife," Zelenin answered. "It got stuck in Yakov's body and it broke, the blade." The Henckel knife was again displayed for the jury.

There was a commotion at the defense table.

Judge Parker interrupted Zelenin. "Let's take a brief recess," Parker said. "Actually, at this point, we'll take our luncheon recess."

Rita Gluzman had collapsed, head in arms, onto the hard wood of the table in front of her, into Rosen's and Hochhesier's hands.

Parker had broken for lunch at the right time. "Just note for the record," the judge told his stenographer, "that at the end of the morning session, around 12:30, the defendant apparently fainted.

"She appears somewhat distraught."

Seventeen

Rita Gluzman's fainting had sent a scary signal to the courtroom observers. It was a bit of drama in a contentious, combative trial. Something had become too much for the widow. Perhaps it had been the retelling of how her husband of twenty-six years had been killed so suddenly by Vladimir Zelenin and her feelings for Yakov had rushed to the surface. Perhaps it was her realization that she had been named so coolly as Zelenin's collaborator, his accomplice in striking the death blow to Yakov, then cutting him up like livestock or a classroom biology experiment. Whatever the case, when the afternoon session began shortly after two, Rita returned with the marshals to Judge Parker's courtroom. After conferring with her lawyers, whom she'd been unable to see during the luncheon recess due to security rules, Rita reassured Larry Hochheiser and Mike Rosen that she was okay. The option existed for her to remain in the holding cell and hear Zelenin's testimony over the in-house television monitor, but Rita mustered the strength to sit at her place at the defense table while Seibel asked Zelenin more about the dismemberment.

The defendant presented a picture of grief to Parker, perhaps the first time she had publicly acted truly bereaved. She told the judge, "It's very difficult for me to hear . . . I would prefer . . . I do not want to watch it on TV, because it was my husband. It was my husband! I'm not going to watch anything about my husband on TV."

As she composed herself, Rita Gluzman was having difficulty breathing. Hochheiser and Rosen tried to help their client, as she told them she was okay to continue. It was a brief scare, as Parker and Seibel watched the defendant seem to fall apart in the middle of Zelenin's testimony.

Sophia Gluzman, Yakov's mother, had been unmoved by her former daughter-in-law's breakdown. "It's a game. She's an actress," she told reporters during the recess.

Zelenin resumed his testimony about the events the night Yakov Gluzman had come home and been greeted with an ax in the face by his wife's cousin. Rita had held a weapon, standing directly in front of her husband as he entered his apartment and she had struck Yakov at the same time Zelenin had. The witness was unsure whether Rita had used the hammer or the smaller ax, but he was certain they struck him in concert. It was probably the ax, Zelenin continued, as the ax had struck his hand, causing the wound in his hand.

Cathy Seibel asked Zelenin what he and Rita had discussed, if anything, while cutting the body and cleaning up. Zelenin told her it was quiet as they worked, and Rita had asked him only when he would be finished.

Zelenin had cut off Yakov's fingertips and ears, to prevent any identification of their victim. It had taken the Russian two or three hours, he said, to finish cutting up the body. There were about sixty pieces. He and Rita put the parts into the heavy duty garbage bags they'd picked up at the Grand Union. Zelenin also put the murder tools into the bags, as well as the cleaning utensils and the cleansing spray.

In the early morning, after packing all the body pieces into the garbage bags, Zelenin had taken the keys to Yakov's Maxima, a couple of the grizzly, reeking trash bags, and gone downstairs to pack a load of human remains into Yakov's car. Unfamiliar with his victim's car, Zelenin unwittingly tripped the Maxima's alarm while putting his first load into the car's trunk. Rita suddenly came running out of the apartment entrance and hustled him into the Maxima, Zelenin told them, and when she started the motor the alarm stopped. They drove off to a bank parking lot down Middletown Road, to park and discuss how they would get the rest of Yakov's body parts out of his apartment. A little while later, Rita dropped him off at the entrance to Celia Gardens. Zelenin continued, and he retrieved his Taurus, then went gently up to Yakov's apartment and brought the remaining bloody trash bags downstairs, placing them in the trunk of his car.

Rita and he had then met down the street on Middletown Road to discuss where they would dump the bags of dissected human remains that had, up until seven hours earlier, been her husband. It was then that the two had arrived at the conclusion to go to ECI's parking lot, a thirty-minute drive south. First, they headed for Zelenin's apartment in Fair Lawn. When they arrived, Rita had gone to CVS, which was three blocks away, for bandages while Zelenin stayed in front of his apartment.

Zelenin checked on his sons, who were still sleeping, got his set of keys to ECI, and continued to the front of CVS, where he met Rita. Rita had yelled at her cousin when she had discovered his headlights weren't working properly on the way to New Jersey. She gave Zelenin a bag containing medication and the bandages she had purchased, and the two drove to ECI, still in their own cars.

Zelenin came to the end of his tale: "We drove towards ECI, but on the way we stopped and were discussing that a certain place would be easier to approach the water. But there were people there, and that's why we decided to drive on further. From there we went to ECI. We drove up to the gates, and discussed what to do further. We agreed that we would leave Yakov's car [at ECI] and that I would drive Rita home, since at that time she had to be home, because at that time Yakov was supposed to come. And she would say, well, she was waiting for him and he didn't come so she left. And I, at the same time, would try to get rid of the bags.

"She gave me the key from the Maxima and I drove her home [to Saddle River]."

Zelenin described how Rita had cut up the credit cards from Yakov's wallet and, with the microcassette recorder from the Pearl River apartment she had used to wiretap her husband, threw them into the trash bags with Yakov's remains. Rita had regretted having to throw out the microcassette recorder, Zelenin said, as she told him it was an expensive item. The special batteries also were expensive, but sadly, they too had to be tossed out. During the 40 minute drive through Bergen County back roads from ECI to Upper Saddle River, Zelenin and Rita talked about how they would meet up after he had finished disposing of the body bags. Zelenin had dropped Rita off, then driven back to ECI, to the rear parking lot, and had begun his dumping chore.

It was beginning to sound like the scene in the movie *Pulp Fiction* where two of the characters need desperately to dispose of a body. Without the professional scrutiny and intervention of Officer Richard Freeman, Rita Gluzman and Vladimir Zelenin might have been as successful as the film characters were.

Cathy Seibel had finished the direct questioning of her star witness. Looking around the courtroom, none of the prosecutors could sense much skepticism about Zelenin's testimony among the spectators or, most importantly, the twelve jurors and Judge Parker. It appeared as though the Russian's words had been accepted. The story was almost too gruesome to have been invented and recited.

Larry Hochheiser would begin his intensive cross-examination. His client's life depended on Hochheiser destroying any credibility Vladimir Zelenin had. Seibel was worried about the autopsy photos and the defense's possible use of them to portray the chief witness against Rita Gluzman as a demonic monster. If Zelenin had gone as far as dissecting someone when he could have simply killed and disposed of his victim without chopping him into little bits, the reasoning went, why would he stop there? After all, his victim had been his benefactor. What would deter him from accusing his victim's wife, implicating her in the gruesome murder?

Hochheiser thought he and Rita were getting a raw deal when the interpreters changed during the break between Cathy Seibel's questioning and his cross-examination. This would grind at the defense lawyers, as the younger Natalia Kavaliauskas replaced the more experienced English-speaker George Markov as the voice of Vladimir Zelenin. But Hochheiser knew he had to play with the cards dealt by the court, and he held his objections. Adding to the defender's angst in getting initial answers from Zelenin was an outburst from the spectator section, from someone who was part of the Israeli contingent of Yakov Gluzman's family. Judge Parker restored order and cautioned the members of the gallery that any further outbursts would cause the marshals to remove them. The atmosphere in the courtroom was tense, and the crowd was anxious to hear the confessed killer's story under fire from Rita Gluzman's lawyers, though some of the crowd probably had heard enough to form an opinion.

Hochheiser went over every detail of Zelenin's statement with the Russian. Did he remember Sergeant Tom Goldrick? Did he remember telling Goldrick the details of the crime Easter Sunday? How had those details changed in the seven months since? When had he last discussed the case and his testimony with Lou Valvo or Cathy Seibel? What kind of deal had he struck with the government? Had he remembered telling Goldrick that he almost attacked Officer Richard Freeman at One Madison? Hochheiser's questions, delivered as rapidly as possible through the interpreter, were intended to trip up Zelenin over any small detail possible that might suggest the prosecution's star witness had rehearsed his testimony, or had changed his statement significantly since the previous April in order to incriminate Rita Gluzman. The Russian was bearing up well under the circumstances: here Rita's lawyer was attacking him, and Zelenin knew he would go to prison for at least twenty years as his situation stood. But the witness answered back calmly. No, I have not changed my testimony. No, I haven't seen Valvo or Seibel, except in court, since they questioned me long before the trial. Yes, I lied through my teeth to immigration, and to others about political asylum, including Goldrick. Yes, I lied about certain events in Kyrgyzstan being anti-Semetic when they weren't.

But Larry Hochheiser's attempts to sully the confessed killer's credibility weren't having their intended effect. Zelenin could have confessed to the killing of President Kennedy, it seemed, and his recollections of Rita Gluzman's participation in the killing of her husband Yakov were still coming across to the court as a truthful statement. Zelenin told Hochheiser how Lou Valvo had hardballed him: even with your testimony, you've got to do twenty, the DA had told him. No deals. All Valvo would agree to do in addition to asking for less than life for Zelenin was to reassure him that his two sons would not be deported. And this, it seemed, was all Vladimir Zelenin really cared about. The safety and security of his sons. That and the possibility of spending the next twenty years of his life, maybe more, at a federal penitentiary in Connecticut or Pennsylvania where his boys could visit him. He hadn't even thought of fighting the arrest in East Rutherford, when he had been caught with both the victim's body and the tools of the crime. Stranger things had happened in American justice through the years than the acquittal of an apparent murderer, one who had seemingly been caught in the act. Yet Zelenin had given in to the authority of Officer Freeman almost at once, like a chess player who concedes his queen when defeat is obvious. He hadn't tried to attack Freeman either.

The rapid-fire cross-examination continued through the afternoon. What school did you get your graduate degree from? How many years were you a teacher? Have you seen a written copy of your guilty plea? Mr. Zelenin, are you able to answer yes or no to these questions? Why was your sentencing in the state court postponed from last September? You weren't yet sentenced to twenty-to-life in state court, were you? You haven't been sentenced in federal court yet either, yes? This jury will never hear what your sentence is, will it? Do you have any idea what the normal time is between a guilty plea and a sentence in federal court without a deal with the government?

Hochheiser was getting frustrated as he dug further into the imperturbable Zelenin: "Where are you in jail now, sir?" the lawyer asked.

"Rockland County jail. Rockland county, jail in Rockland."

"And you live alone there? I mean, do you have your own cage?"

"Yes, I'm alone in my cell."

"And did you see anybody from the prosecutor's office over the weekend?"

"No."

"What time did you get here and what time do you go back?"

"Well, I was brought here around lunchtime, and I go back around five."

"Are you telling us that you came into this courtroom without preparing your testimony with the prosecutor?"

"Yes. [But] I want to say that I was asked questions regarding my case and I answered those questions."

"When?" Hochheiser continued. "Where did this meeting take place?"

"In the office of the district attorney," Zelenin replied.

Hochheiser asked about Zelenin's wardrobe. Why was he wearing this nice wool suit, and not his prison jumpsuit? Had the government bought him this suit, to dress him up, make the killer appear presentable to the jury?

"This is my own suit," Zelenin replied. "This suit

came here from Gomel in Byelorussia." There was some laughter as the witness referred to his faraway tailor.

Hochheiser asked Zelenin to retell the crime, his killing of Yakov. "How many pieces did you cut Yakov into? Was it more than ten? Was it more than 100?"

Cathy Seibel had worried about the defense attorneys demonizing her witness by showing the jury the autopsy photos of Yakov Gluzman. Zelenin was barbaric, to be sure, she had admitted as much in her opening statement. The witness was a ruthless, desperate, butcher of another human being.

But there was a reverse effect on the courtroom spectators, many of whom were friends or had been family of Yakov Gluzman. Rather than vent their anger at Zelenin, they were hissing at Rita Gluzman from their seats, even with Judge Parker's warnings. Zelenin was being viewed as a messenger, rather than as an active participant, and this bothered Hochheiser and Rosen, who felt their client was being beaten up as she sat at the defense table. The fainting, combined with Rita's fatigue throughout the afternoon during the retelling of her husband's murder, was having a bad effect on Rita's health and ability to stay alert during the testimony. Parker adjourned for the day, sending Zelenin back to his Rockland jail cell and Rita to Valhalla.

As the third day of Zelenin's testimony began, Mike Rosen asked for a moment with Judge Parker: the lawyer wanted the judge to declare a mistrial. Rosen's reasoning was simple: the government hadn't fully disclosed their star witness Vladimir Zelenin's "prior bad acts" as fully as Seibel had claimed. While Rosen and Hochheiser had been working late at Hochheiser's Westchester County home preparing their questions, they'd received a fax from Rosen's law office in lower Manhattan. It was an eight-page memorandum from Deirdre

Daly and Cathy Seibel providing the defense with the government's obligatory "Brady" and "Giglio" disclosures about inconsistencies in Zelenin's prior statements since the time of his arrest and listing the previous dishonest statements he'd made, such as those on the immigration forms. The Brady provision covers "exculpatory facts" and the Giglio covers the "prior bad acts" of a witness that affect credibility. Rosen was incensed that he and Hochheiser had received the memo only, it seemed, at the eleventh hour. Accusing Daly and Seibel of "prosecutorial misconduct," Rosen tried to show Judge Parker how Zelenin's credibility was damaged to the extent that nothing the witness said should be accepted in Parker's court. Neither Rosen nor Hochheiser had received all the discovery information until the beginning of the trial. "It would have affected Hochheiser's opening!" Rosen told Parker. Neither attorney had been able to compare Zelenin's original statements to Sgt. Tom Goldrick with what the prisoner had told Lou Valvo and Cathy Seibel until after Rita Gluzman's trial had begun. It had put the defense at a disadvantage, Rosen said.

The defense's complaints, grounded in some fact, amounted to little in the way of substance. The defense lawyers knew what Zelenin had told the prosecutors before the trial began, and were complaining that they weren't able to detect the nuances and subtle changes, in the killer's statements from Easter Sunday until early January, items that might have changed upon reflection, such as how premeditated the crime was, or what Rita was wearing.

Seibel had followed the law assiduously, and had turned over all materials due the defense, including the form 3500 crucial to explaining Zelenin's inconsistencies, within the time limit set by federal law. They had resent the material to the defense prior to cross examination. The prosecutor went on to explain to Parker the ludicrousness of Rosen's application for a mistrial and how there was little that was left out of Zelenin's "Giglio" and "Brady" statements. The 3500 forms came under the "Tome" provisions governing prior consistent statements by witnesses. "He knew it existed," Seibel told Parker. "He knew before he opened that this material was coming."

Parker seemed skeptical of Rosen's and Hochheiser's claims to have been unaware of the subtle changes in Zelenin's testimony over the seven months the man was in custody. Zelenin had first told Goldrick he and Rita had killed Yakov spontaneously, then later admitted to Goldrick and Lou Valvo they had planned the murder three weeks before. It was this inconsistency Rita's lawyers said they had just learned, while Rosen and Hochheiser claimed the government was setting Rita up using her cousin's testimony. If Zelenin had confessed to Goldrick on Easter Sunday and only later told the investigators Rita had been involved, the lawyers would have had a good point. In both statements, though, Zelenin had clearly implicated Rita Gluzman. Rosen and Hochheiser wanted to get the case thrown out of court. But Judge Parker had seen and heard just about everything in his time and, while retaining the air of impartiality necessary to run his courtroom, would not disqualify Zelenin or declare a mistrial.

Moreover, Seibel had not been required by law to provide to the defense the two minor attachments to Zelenin's prior statements Rita's lawyers complained about not receiving.

"This is no shock to the defense," said Seibel. "They opened knowing Rita was implicated the first day."

Parker ruled the issue a moot point, and told the

attorneys to continue their cross-examination of Zelenin.

For the better part of the morning, Hochheiser reviewed nearly every detail of each report in which Zelenin was questioned the day of his arrest. Did you say this? Do you remember saying that? How did you cut yourself? Do you remember telling the paramedic you cut yourself? Will you tell us again what you claim in this courtroom happened when Yakov Gluzman walked in the door of his apartment? Did you ever tell anybody that you used this little ax and that Rita Gluzman used this big ax, or do you claim that Rita used the little ax and you used the big ax? Do you remember the time and place you were arrested?

Hochheiser was again trying to trip up Zelenin, in any way possible, over the killer's recollections. And the lawyer was making no progress in proving Zelenin a liar on the stand. The constant translation was frustrating to Hochheiser, and Zelenin was unable to answer most of the lawyer's questions with a "yes" or "no." By the end of the morning session, Hochheiser had asked Zelenin almost a hundred questions concerning the ax used as the murder weapon, whether he was sure Rita had bought it at the Home Depot, whether she had paid cash, what sort of handle the ax had, how he had struck Yakov Gluzman, and so on. Zelenin proved to be a strong witness, invulnerable to the badgering by the defense.

Hochheiser reviewed the other details. Had Zelenin remembered the phone call he had told the police he and Rita had made from the pay phone at the 7-11? Had he heard Yakov Gluzman's phone ring during the evening while he lay in wait for the biologist to return from work? The phone company records had shown an incoming call to the Pearl River apartment. What did he do when he heard the phone ring? Had he made a phone call out, using Yakov's phone?

By now Parker was tiring of the relentless, meticulous cross-examination of Zelenin. "How much longer?" the judge asked Hochheiser.

"I don't know," Hochheiser responded. "Hopefully I'm almost done. I'm not repeating anything."

"I beg to differ," Seibel interrupted.

"I'm not really repeating anything," Hochheiser told Parker and Seibel. "I'm doing it by categories and items that are listed. I'm going through them, just that there are so many of them."

"How long is your list?" Parker asked.

"My list is about five feet long, literally, five feet long," Rita's lawyer told the judge.

"We're beyond four feet now, are we?" Parker asked, dryly.

Hochheiser sensed the judge's impatience. "I think so."

Parker summed up his observations. "I'm concerned. I'll give the jury a break now, but they're starting to fidget, and they're starting to look somewhat distracted. I'm not sure ten minutes on this phone call—" but the judge was interrupted by Hochheiser.

"My problem is—"

"I'm sorry?" the judge asked.

"My problem is, it was a simple question," Hochheiser continued. "Was there a phone call made from the apartment? The guy starts telling me about phone calls made into the apartment or pretends not to know what I'm talking about. He's got two interpreters standing next to him. He put me in a position. It took me a long time to get a simple answer to a simple question."

The language barrier was now exhausting Hochheiser to the point of aggravation. "The process of an interpreter itself, it more than doubles the time!'' he told Parker.

But the judge's patience was being challenged, and he reminded Hochheiser that the attorney was wrapping up his cross-examination of Zelenin.

Vladimir Zelenin's story had indeed changed, with respect to mostly minor details, in the period from his first statement to Sergeant Goldrick on April 7 to his initial interview with the prosecution on April 26. It was only during the later meeting that he'd told the investigators of his and Rita's journey to her home in the middle of the night, when she had cleaned up and changed clothes. It was details such as that one that bothered Rosen and Hochheiser, who felt the government had steered Zelenin toward implicating Rita and had allowed him to change his statement, adding details that incriminated his cousin, during the first month he was in custody.

There was also the matter of Zelenin's hand wound, which had occurred, he said, during the killing of Yakov Gluzman. Zelenin had told Goldrick and the other investigators differing versions of how he dressed the wound, though it was uncontested that Rita had purchased the bandages found in Zelenin's car and used on his cut, and she had bought them on Sunday morning. That had been another apparent inconsistency that had bothered Rosen and Hochheiser.

Rita Gluzman's education as a chemist was brought in, almost as an aside, by Hochheiser. Did Zelenin tell the investigators that he had seen Rita washing the gray sweatpants she'd worn the night of the murder when she and Zelenin had gone to her home in the middle of the night? Hadn't he also told them that Rita added Clorox bleach to the wash, to clean the blood out of the sweatpants? If so, wouldn't that be stupid? Hochheiser implied. Certainly a chemist such as Rita would know not to add bleach to a wash consisting of gray sweatpants.

But Zelenin told Hochheiser that he had told the investigators only that Rita had washed the sweatpants. He couldn't recall whether she had added Clorox, though he had suggested it to Rita as a way of getting the blood out permanently.

There was Gregory Kogan, the other cousin, from Brooklyn. Vladimir Zelenin had testified he had paid $2,000 to stop Kogan from reporting the terrified Zelenin to the INS. Hochheiser implied that the amount paid to Kogan was more than $2,000, and that his owing Yakov Gluzman more money was enough motive for Zelenin to have killed Yakov Gluzman on his own.

"Did anyone ever tell you," Hochheiser asked Zelenin, "that they listened to a tape-recorded conversation which suggests you owed Yakov Gluzman about $10,000?"

"Never did we have such conversations." Zelenin replied through the interpreter.

"Did Yakov Gluzman ever pay Gregory Kogan money in your behalf?"

"On my behalf? No."

"Did Yakov Gluzman, sir, pay Gregory Kogan money because [Kogan] told Yakov Gluzman that you owed a corrupt INS official named Vitaly?"

"Yakov loaned money to me . . . to give it to Gregory."

"Sir, there came a time when you understood that Yakov Gluzman discovered that you and Gregory Kogan were shaking him down in the name of a fictitious, corrupt, INS official named Vitaly, isn't that right, sir?"

Cathy Seibel objected to Hochheiser's line of questioning, but Parker overruled the prosecutor. For fans of reasonable doubt, the suggestion of an alliance between Zelenin and Gregory Kogan, not Rita Gluzman, at least seemed possible, were it not for the circumstantial evidence the prosecutors had introduced supporting Zelenin's testimony about Rita.

But Hochheiser was unfazed. He wanted to show the jury, which had not yet seen the autopsy photos, the gruesome photographs of the body parts laying on the medical examiner's table, but was reluctant to do so. The strategy could backfire if the jury thought Rita had participated in the grisly dismemberment. Hochheiser wanted the jurors to understand, however, the result of Zelenin's cutting up of Yakov Gluzman and the surgically precise manner in which the admitted killer had cut up his victim's body.

Hochheiser's attack on the government's chief witness and alleged co-conspirator could not rest unless the lawyer was able to show Zelenin's apparent ruthless butchery of Yakov Gluzman.

"Sir, you gave us reasons that you cut up Yakov Gluzman and killed [him]. Isn't there an additional reason you hated the man?" Hochheiser asked. "Now, you were asked by the investigators about how you cut up the body, isn't that right? Yes?"

"Yes."

"And they asked you why you actually removed each organ, like the heart and the liver and the lungs, the intestines, like surgically. They asked you about that?"

"Yes."

"But there was one thing that they were particularly interested in, wasn't it?"

Seibel objected and requested a sidebar. The prosecutor knew where Hochheiser was headed with his questioning of Zelenin.

At the sidebar, Parker was curious. "What are you about to ask?" the judge questioned Hochheiser.

"[Zelenin] did a strange thing because, aside from

cutting everything into small pieces, he did one very strange thing that the investigators picked up on also. He cut the genital areas in one piece with the pubic hair, the penis, the scrotum and the testicles all together as though there was some particular design to it," Hochheiser told the judge and Seibel. "It wasn't like the rest of the cutting, and [the investigators] realized it was something strange that might suggest some motive and so do I. I wish to bring it out. I'm not trying to introduce a photograph or anything gruesome like that. [But] I think it does go to motive and I think I'm derelict if I don't ask."

"What are you going to ask?" Parker calmly inquired.

"I'm going to ask him exactly that. [Why] he cut the genitalia in this particular way. He did it carefully."

Seibel tried to downplay any special significance of Zelenin's trimming of Yakov Gluzman's genitals. "Your Honor, there are myriad ways to inquire . . . about the number of pieces he cut the body into, and about whether he did this out of some animus toward the victim . . . and I don't think it's probative of anything," the prosecutor argued to Parker.

"What are you afraid of?" Hochheiser asked Seibel and Daly.

"We're not afraid of anything," Daly cooly retorted to the defender.

Parker supervised. "What is it probative of?" the judge asked.

"It's probative of the fact he has to harbor some hatred for this guy," Hochheiser answered. "[Zelenin] had his own agenda. He wasn't going to dispose of this body."

Parker wanted the trial to proceed, and felt the cross-examination of Zelenin was already too long, entering its third day. "I'll give you another ten or fifteen minutes to wrap this up," the judge told Hochheiser, staying an opinion on the replaying of the genital carving by Zelenin. "I'm giving you a lot of latitude with this witness."

"You've been generous," Hochheiser replied.

"That will be an issue we will certainly revisit if need be," came Parker's reply, as bold a double-meaning as the soft-spoken jurist had stated in the two weeks.

Zelenin returned for his third day of testimony to face Mike Rosen and Larry Hochheiser in a state of heightened anger. The attorneys were still miffed over the form 3500 problem, which they had told Parker caught them off guard unfairly before they began their cross-examination of the government witness who most threatened their client's freedom. Rosen had argued to Parker for a mistrial, certain that the prosecution had somehow sandbagged the defense lawyers.

But Parker had reviewed the inconsistencies in the 3500 statements and concluded that there was little substantial change in Zelenin's comments to Goldrick, Valvo, and the others over the month and a half he had told the investigators about the night of the killing. There would be no cause for mistrial, the judge informed Rosen.

The lawyers were going to take a final shot at Zelenin. Hochheiser decided to delve further into the witness' dissection of Yakov Gluzman's body and genital region.

"Do you remember," Hochheiser asked Zelenin, "that you cut the genitalia in a special way, so that the pubic hair, the penis, the scrotum, and the testicles were not cut into pieces, but were kept carefully in one nice display? Do I have to show you a picture?"

Zelenin answered as though he were a kosher butcher. "I hadn't any experience with cutting human bodies, but from my knowledge of cutting animals, I knew that the proper way would be so that I do not touch the intestines," he told Hochheiser.

"You removed the heart in one piece, didn't you?"

"I was simply cutting it. I did not think at that time how I was doing it."

Hochheiser had a point to prove. "Did they ask you if you did that out of hatred, or some other state of mind, toward Yakov Gluzman?" the lawyer asked, referring to the prior interviews with the detectives.

"They did ask me," Zelenin answered.

"Did they ask you if perhaps your accomplice had suggested that these genitalia be cut in this special way? Did they ask you that, sir?"

"I don't recall them asking this," Zelenin replied. "But I did not have any hatred, or, as you put it, state of mind towards Yakov. I was doing that purely mechanically. I knew that I was doing something awful, but I did not have any particular thoughts as to the method of doing that."

Seated next to her lawyer, Rita Gluzman gasped repeatedly as Zelenin recalled how he had dissected her husband so clinically. The gallery behind her, comprised of Yakov Gluzman's family, looked angrily at her.

Hochheiser questioned Zelenin about his other actions the night of the murder, including whether the man had used Yakov's telephone to call ECI. The lawyer was pulling out all possible stops to suggest the witness had an accomplice other than Rita, and in each question Hochheiser reminded the jury and Zelenin of his violent crime. "At the time you drove an ax in Yakov Gluzman's head, you had health insurance and dental insurance from ECI, is that correct, sir?" Unless he could fully demonize Zelenin, impeaching the man's testimony in front of the jury would be difficult.

Hochheiser and Rosen both thought that Gregory

Kogan had played a larger role in the case than Zelenin had admitted. Hochheiser suggested the two Kyrgyz cousins had concocted a scheme to defraud Yakov using an immigration agent, and that both men had tried to shake down the wealthier and more successful Yakov by telling the scientist there was imminent peril to them if they didn't come up with $10,000. Zelenin denied participating in any scheme, but didn't put it past Kogan to have approached Yakov for more money than Zelenin had already paid the Brooklyn cousin. Hochheiser couldn't get the witness to budge at all.

The lawyer then returned to Zelenin's prior statements. Hadn't he told Tom Goldrick that cutting Yakov into pieces was a decision he and his accomplice had made spontaneously, after they had killed Yakov? And hadn't he seemed to contradict this first statement when, in talks with the Rockland district attorneys in May, he told Lou Valvo that Rita and he had decided before they went to Pearl River they would dissect the man? Hochheiser tried with each question to leave the impression on the jurors that the government's representatives had coached Zelenin and told the prisoner to change his story to appear that Rita was involved in a premeditated murder.

In his conversations with Rita Gluzman in the month before Yakov's death, hadn't Zelenin discussed Yakov's insurance policies with her, Hochheiser wanted to know. And had he encouraged or discouraged her? Didn't he know that if Yakov disappeared, Rita would most likely have to wait years to collect insurance payments?

Zelenin acknowledged the insurance discussions, and had pointed out to Rita, he said, the difficulty in collecting without a body. It wasn't what the lawyer wanted to hear.

Defense attorney Hochheiser's cross-examination continued throughout the morning, despite Judge Parker's instructions to wrap it up quickly. But Parker was patient.

Did he have any understanding on April 7 as to any benefit to him if he had implicated another person? Did he have any reason to implicate someone else? What were your first thoughts upon seeing the police officer? Hochheiser continued.

"When I saw the policeman for the first time, my thoughts were how I could flee," Zelenin told him. "But I understood it was impossible, that it was futile, so I didn't do it."

"And when you were arrested, did you know what sentence you were facing?"

"At the moment I was arrested, I thought it was going to be capital punishment."

Seibel had to show the jury that Zelenin understood he would be granted some leniency from his anticipated death sentence by testifying against Rita Gluzman, even if he hadn't actually been facing capital punishment, and that Parker would be the arbiter of his truthfulness in deciding whether the witness would see his sentence reduced to twenty or so years. Then she introduced the inconsistencies, and asked Zelenin to explain them.

"When you met with investigators or prosecutors, did anybody tell you whether a particular meeting was part of the investigation or part of your trial testimony in preparation?"

"Nobody told me that this was preparation for some trial. I was told it was part of the investigation and it was necessary for me to tell the truth."

Hochheiser interjected, saying that Zelenin's answer didn't conform to the wording of Seibel's question.

"We all heard the question, Mr. Hochheiser," the

judge admonished him. "If you have an objection, lodge your objection."

"I object, Your Honor," came Hochheiser's response.

"Sustained." The judge was a man who kept to the letter of his courtroom rules.

Seibel rephrased her question. "You were shown by Mr. Hochheiser various reports by various investigators. Before taking the stand, had you ever viewed those reports?"

"I haven't reviewed the reports," Zelenin answered.

There was also the question of which murder weapon Zelenin had used. There were two axes, one with a long handle, one with a shorter handle. Zelenin said he had sawed off this handle so that Rita could use it. At first, Zelenin had said he'd used the shorter ax, to Tom Goldrick. Later, he told Lou Valvo he used the longer one. Parker was interested in the specifics of the axes. Seibel wanted to pre-empt Hochheiser's use of the inconsistency and asked for redirect, which the judge granted.

"Tell us again who used which ax?" the prosecutor asked.

"During the attack on Yakov, I used the bigger ax, the one with the wooden handle. When I was handling Yakov's body, I was using the smaller ax."

Hochheiser was frustrated, and asked Zelenin if he had lied to Tom Goldrick about which ax he'd used.

"I don't recall telling the sergeant I used a different ax," Zelenin said.

Seibel asked Zelenin what was in it for him? What did he expect to get from testifying here?

"As far as I understand, irrespective of what the court decides in relation to Rita Gluzman, and irrespective of what the court decides as to how I have fulfilled the provisions of that agreement, the government will appeal to the judge so that I would be granted some benefits."

"And what are the consequences if you do not tell the truth in your testimony?" Seibel continued.

Zelenin paused to grasp the U.S. Attorney's question. "Well, my understanding is that the agreement would be annulled," he said.

"And regardless of what the government puts in its letter to Judge Parker, it is Judge Parker who will decide your sentence, right?"

"As far as I understand, yes."

Seibel continued her redirect. What had Rita told him about alimony, while they were preparing to kill Yakov?

"The defendant said that at that time was a good time to get rid of Yakov because [she] made an application for alimony. It was quite a substantial amount and [she inferred] people may think that he was afraid of alimony and fled somewhere."

"What was your understanding," Seibel asked Zelenin, "about what would have happened if Gregory Kogan or Rita Gluzman or anyone else told the Immigration Service that you had lied in your asylum application?"

"I think I would have been deported."

"The defendant knew that there were false statements in your application, did she not?"

"Yes. She did know. She was aware of the threats that Gregory Kogan was making."

"And she herself had made a false statement in your asylum application?"

Hochheiser was fuming. He requested a conference with Parker and Seibel.

"The door was opened, Your Honor," Seibel suggested to Parker. "She submitted a false affidavit on his behalf. I asked Mr. Hochheiser before I questioned Zelenin if he was going to touch on it, and he said he wouldn't. I said therefore I wouldn't. [But] he did touch on it. He opened the door when he suggested that Zelenin knew he couldn't be deported because he had asylum status and then said Rita Gluzman knew he couldn't be deported because he had asylum status. He asked those questions about Rita Gluzman's familiarity with immigration matters because ECI handled immigration matters for its employees and he suggested that his client had no reason to think that Mr. Zelenin was in a danger of being deported."

Cathy Seibel competed her linkage. "I am entitled to bring out that she knew he was in danger of being deported because she knew he made false statements in the application because she made a false statement on his behalf. When she is talking to the witness about doing the murder and saying 'I'll help you with your immigration problem if you help me with the Yakov problem,' the witness knew that she had something on him, that there were false statements and that he was at risk of being deported despite his political asylum status. The misleading impression has been left on [Hochheiser's cross-examination] that he was not deportable because he had no asylum."

Hochheiser was still fuming. "She was going to tell on herself that she committed perjury and then she was going to get herself arrested to get him deported?" he quizzically asked Parker. "The only thing that could be said about your argument," he told Seibel, "is that it is imaginative. It is disingenuous . . ."

Parker cut Hochheiser off. "What is your substantive response to it?"

"My response," Hochheiser continued, "is this is a [prior] bad act of Rita Gluzman. I never opened the door with it. This is an imaginative argument, but has no substance whatsoever."

Parker told the attorneys to get to the point with Zelenin.

"At the time you discussed committing the murder with the defendant," Seibel asked the witness, "did you believe your asylum status was at risk?"

"Yes."

Seibel went through Zelenin's testimony exhaustively on her redirect examination. What about the phone card Rita borrowed from you [to call Burton] that was registered to her mother at your apartment? What gloves were you wearing? Which ax did you use? What about Gregory Kogan? How much did you borrow from Yakov?

Hochheiser followed Seibel's redirect with his own questions about Zelenin's motives. Wasn't he trying to find a bigger apartment? How would he afford such a place on his $8 per hour job? What was he going to do to earn more money? Into the afternoon, Rita's lawyer hammered away at Zelenin, but was unable to trip the witness up in a way that caused him to contradict anything he had said in three and a half days on the stand.

Finally, Parker thanked Zelenin and excused him from the stand. As he got up to face the court officer to be handcuffed, Zelenin turned to his cousin at the defense table.

"Fuck you, bitch!" he shouted angrily at Rita Gluzman.

Zelenin hadn't bothered to use the interpreter for his closing remark.

The most important testimony in the trial of US v. Rita Gluzman had come to its conclusion after nearly four days.

Eighteen

Deirdre Daly and Cathy Seibel continued to call supporting witnesses after Vladimir Zelenin's emotional testimony. Insurance claims investigators testified about Yakov Gluzman's policies and how the policies would have been paid to Rita even if Yakov had been missing, after three years or so in accordance with New Jersey laws and the filing of a presumptive death certificate there by Yakov's survivors. Igor Zelenin, at seventeen the youngest of the witnesses, verified his father's visit the morning after the crime [when he was on his way to East Rutherford] to check in on his sons.

The jury was given David Rom's deposition videotaped in Israel and watched the Israeli private investigator recount how it had been Rita Gluzman who had hired him to tail Yakov Gluzman and Raisa Korenblit, and how Rita had asked for the photos in late September, telling the investigator to use her Federal Express account to rush her the photos of her husband and the younger woman. One of these photos turned up at the Hadera police station in the extortion case.

The next emotional testimony, and the one that would cause the greatest rift between the prosecutors and Rita's defense lawyers, came as Seibel called Ilan Gluzman to the stand.

At twenty-six, Ilan had matured quickly, and was now faced with the tortuous task of telling the court how his mother had expected his father at Upper Saddle River Easter Sunday morning to pick up his remaining belongings. That morning, the last time he saw his mother before she fled, Ilan told the jurors that she said she thought Yakov wouldn't come after all for his things, because he hadn't called to confirm. It was 7 A.M. Ilan was terse in his recollections, glancing at his mother only occasionally as he testified.

But Hochheiser had opened a past wound when he cross-examined Ilan. Hadn't he sent his father an angry letter a year ago? Wasn't Yakov abusive toward his son? Didn't Ilan say in his letter to Yakov, "Next time you attack me, I'll hit you so hard you'll have to kill me?"

At their table, Daly and Seibel were angered by Hochheiser's inference. The lawyer's next question really upset the prosecutors.

"Where were you on Saturday night?"

Ilan had been on a date, in Staten Island, he told them, and had been out so late that he'd pulled over, tired, on the New Jersey Turnpike to rest, falling asleep for several hours before returning to Upper Saddle River in the early hours of Sunday morning.

The damage was done. Daly was furious that Hochheiser, acting on Rita's behalf, would imply that her son was somehow involved in the killing of his father.

* * *

Dr. Mary Anne Clayton was one of the last witnesses. The autopsy of Yakov Gluzman was the most challenging of her career, she said. She had established that Yakov was killed by a blow from an instrument such as an ax, but couldn't be certain of the time of death. The body had been chopped into so many pieces, it had been impossible to tell if rigor mortis had set in when she first saw the body parts. Because of the seating arrangements in the federal courtroom, Clayton found herself just several feet away from Rita Gluzman, who was again gasping as the medical examiner explained what she'd been faced with. Clayton was grateful she hadn't had to testify too long, though she'd had to wait almost a day to get to the stand.

Sergeant Tom Goldrick's appearance was short. He recalled the events of Easter Sunday, and how Vladimir Zelenin had quickly volunteered that Rita Gluzman had killed Yakov with him. The defense attorneys excused the detective with little cross-examination.

Finally, Deirdre Daly called an old friend of Rita's, Gary Schnayderman, an engineer from Chicago. He had gone out on several "dates," he said, with Rita Gluzman. The two had seen one another four years earlier, long before Rita and Yakov had separated. Evidently, Rita had liked Schnayderman, as she gave the man a gift after several of their dates. What had she given him? Daly inquired.

A set of Henckel knives, he told the courtroom.

After three weeks of prosecution witnesses, fifty-five in all, Larry Hochheiser and Mike Rosen prepared for the closing arguments. They still could not provide an alibi for Rita's wherabouts on Saturday night, and had been unable to damage Zelenin. The confessed killer had come across as contrite for his role in killing Yakov, and had communicated his disdain for Rita and her duress, the threats she had made to him, and the notion that he knew his life was over.

Nineteen

The trial was winding down, ahead of Judge Parker's schedule, and the final two days of summation would either close the case for the prosecutors or allow Rosen and Hochheiser, two trial lawyers with years of heated courtroom arguments behind them, the opportunity to put Zelenin in a more demonic light.

Cathy Seibel had given the prosecution's opening argument, a spectacular statement that had introduced the government's case against Rita Gluzman in a way that had left Hochheiser and Rosen grasping for any technicality possible during the two weeks that would enable the defenders to move for a mistrial. That would have been the only case possible to acquit Rita in the federal trial, as the paper trail of circumstantial evidence combined with Zelenin's testimony had caused the widow of Yakov Gluzman to appear as though she had been less than a passive spectator in her husband's killing. The witnesses introduced into the record, along with the phone records and Rita's disappearance at a time when only Yakov's murderer would have known he was dead, had crippled the defense.

Rita's cold demeanor at the defense table hadn't helped her at all with the jury. She had come across "as sympathetic as one of the Nuremberg defendants," a reporter observed, in both her poise and facial expressions. And she hadn't taken the stand, which, even with the benefit of doubt granted by the law and the court, hadn't allowed her to establish any direct rapport with the seven men and five women who would decide her fate. All the jurors had seen was a hostile, angry defendant who seemed offended at having to be there at all on trial, rather than one whose innocence might have been communicated better to the panel. Her gasps when hearing how her husband had been butchered had seemed disingenuous to observers.

Still, the prosecution needed to reinforce for the jury the overwhelming evidence against Rita Gluzman, so Deirdre Daly's closing summation needed to match in its veracity Cathy Seibel's opening remarks. Knowing that Rosen, who'd gotten other defendants acquitted in similar cases, was set to deliver the defense's summation added to Daly's need for a conclusive statement from the prosecution.

Rosen tried before Daly's summation to have the testimony of Gary Schnayderman, the old friend Rita had dated, struck from the record. He and Hochheiser argued before Parker that the jury might have concluded that Rita had actually committed adultery even before she and Yakov had filed for divorce, thus negating any success by the defense counsel to show that it had been Yakov who had been promiscuous and a philanderer. The lawyers again asked for a mistrial. Seibel and Daly told Rosen, Hochheiser, and Parker in a sidebar that the prosecutors hadn't planned to reiterate Schnayderman's testimony, and Parker refused to strike the witness's earlier comments about having "dated" Rita Gluzman from the record. The jury could infer what it wished from the seemingly innocent statements. Certainly there were no grounds for a mistrial, Parker told them, even under the strictest rules of trial testimony.

Parker knew how to banter with Rosen and Hochheiser. At one point prior to Daly's summation, the judge and the attorneys had a ten-minute discussion without the jury present on the meaning of adultery, each presenting a viewpoint of interpretation, in regard to Schnayderman's reference to his and Rita "dating." Parker told the lawyers that someone simply hearing of a man and woman knowing each other socially wouldn't necessarily infer the two were having a sexual relationship, telling them that "people who take [adultery] seriously are not likely to make that kind of speculation."

Rosen had been more sensitive to the possible impact of Schnayderman's off-the-cuff remark, arguing that the jury members' minds would be poisoned toward Rita at this late hour. "Apparently the press heard [Schnayderman's comment] and we're concerned that if the press heard it, the jury heard it," Rosen explained.

"The more seriously you take adultery," the judge had explained, "the less likely you are to infer that somebody is doing it on the basis of a casual remark. I know we have different takes on this."

Rosen had little choice but to smile, and finished his explanation to the judge. "And that's why it's a great country." His attempt to exclude Schnayderman's comments or to have a mistrial declared were fruitless, but now was not the time to alienate the judge.

"You've been around a long time," Parker said.

Now the jury entered the courtroom, and Deirdre Daly rose to deliver the government's conclusion, to drive the last nail through Rita Gluzman's coffin.

"When this case began," Daly told the jury, "Mr. Hochheiser suggested that this case was about winning, that the government would do anything to win. Ladies and gentlemen, this case is not about winning. This case is about justice. It's about the tragic, senseless, brutal, coldblooded murder of a good man, a brilliant scientist, a man who did nothing to deserve what this defendant did to him. The evidence in this case," Daly continued, "has showed that this defendant planned [Yakov's] murder, executed his murder, and fled in hopes of escaping the responsibility for that murder, and, ladies and gentlemen, the government submits that this defendant must be held accountable for that murder."

It should be noted that not once in the opening of her summation did Daly elect to apologize to the jury for having brought Rita Gluzman to trial, or for wanting to see the widow found guilty and imprisoned for the rest of her life. There were no protesters outside on Quarropas Street, demanding "justice for Rita," and the few television cameras outside on the courthouse steps focused more on the sensational nature of the crime and on Rita's poor showing in front of the jury than on other, distracting issues.

"Now," Daly continued, "what has the evidence shown you? It has shown that this defendant was enraged and panicked by the fact that her husband was going to leave her, no longer giving her money to keep ECI going, no longer supporting her lifestyle or putting up with her arguing and her insults. He was getting out, starting over, starting a new life with Raisa Korenblit in Israel, and Rita Gluzman would not have that. So she recorded his telephone calls, she sent him and his family threatening letters extorting money from him, and when neither of these things worked, she recruited Vladimir Zelenin, who felt himself entirely dependent on her, and together with Zelenin's help she murdered her husband."

If there were any questions in any juror's mind as to whether the U.S. Attorney had second thoughts about Rita's participation in Yakov's murder, they were erased after five minutes of Deirdre Daly's summation.

"The government didn't choose Vladimir Zelenin as a witness," Daly continued. "This defendant chose Vladimir Zelenin, and she chose him because he was the one person in the world who she could control best. A man who depended on her for everything. She had given him a job, an apartment for his sons, a car, and the ability to live in America, and she knew he feared that if he didn't help her, she would send him back to Russia.

"Did that justify what he did? Of course not. But the point is that this defendant was confident when she recruited Vladimir Zelenin that he would agree to help her kill Yakov. Don't misunderstand," Daly continued. "The government does not embrace this man. What Zelenin did will never be forgiven in his life. We told you from the outset that he had committed incredibly unspeakable acts, but the government must take its witnesses as it finds them, and who is really going to know about a horrific crime like this other than someone who had participated in it?"

Explaining why the prosecutors relied on Zelenin, Daly explained to the jury that, "What the government did is what the government should have done. They investigated. They interrogated Zelenin to see if his statements were truthful, and they went out in search of other evidence which would indicate whether he was telling the truth or whether he was not telling the truth. And when they found that evidence, it supported and corroborated what Zelenin had told them."

After reviewing Officer Richard Freeman's discovery of Zelenin the previous Easter Sunday, and the articles recovered from his Taurus, including the damning cassettes from Rita Gluzman's tape recorder, the CVS bandages, and the sliced-up credit cards, Daly launched into a review of Rita's disappearance. "The defendant fled. She was nowhere to be found. She wasn't at home consoling her son, who had so tragically lost his father. She wasn't with her family or her employees. A full-scale national hunt was conducted. It took six days to find her. And where was she? Holed up in Cold Spring Harbor, dying her hair, reading travel books, calling airlines, using aliases when she contacted people, and driving around in a car with stolen license plates on it so that she wouldn't be identified. Are these the actions of an innocent grieving widow?" Daly asked. "Of course not. "They are the actions of a killer on the run.

"And what did the investigation uncover? Theresa and John Smith, Yakov Gluzman's neighbors who lived in the apartment next to him ... testified that they heard a loud thump on the night of the murder, and the following morning they saw a man and a woman walking out of Celia Gardens and getting into Yakov's Nissan. There is no question that it was a woman. They knew it was a woman by her coat, by the way she walked, and by her stature.

"Now, ladies and gentlemen, what other woman in the world would have been with Vladimir Zelenin that night killing Yakov Gluzman? None other than this defendant. And what else did the investigation reveal? That if the defendant had succeeded in her cool plan, she, not Vladimir Zelenin or anyone else, would have ultimately received assets over $1.7 million. Plenty of money to pay off her mortgage and to keep ECI afloat for a long time, just like she told Vladimir Zelenin."

Deirdre Daly was succinct, cool, and confident as she delivered her summation of Rita Gluzman's guilt to the jury, uninterrupted by anyone at the defense table. She then came to the summit of her presentation.

"Then there were the weapons," the prosecutor continued. "The Henckel knife found with the knives in Zelenin's Taurus. Henckel is this defendant's brand of knife. It's not Vladimir Zelenin's brand of knife. This defendant gave her friend, Gary Schnayderman, a Henckel knife. This defendant had a block of Henckel knives on her kitchen counter and additional Henckel knives in her drawers. Is it a cosmic coincidence that the murder weapon in this case is this defendant's brand of knife? Of course not!" Daly told the jury. Leaving out the discovery of the Henckel knives found with Rita at Cold Spring Harbor, and not needing to remind the jury that the tip of the shorter Henckel knife had remained in Yakov Gluzman's arm after slicing it from his torso, Daly had gotten her point across to the jury, which had probably not been very familiar three weeks before with brand-name knives such as the designer Henckels so prevalent in the case of U.S. vs. Rita Gluzman.

Daly then got to the root of Rita's relationship with Yakov, retracing the couple's courtship, emigration, and marriage for the jury. Relating Michael Gluzman's testimony about Rita's abusiveness toward his brother, and capitalizing on the younger Gluzman's dislike for his longtime sister-in-law, Daly told the jury to "step back for a minute and start at the beginning. Michael Gluzman . . . testified that in 1969 Yakov and the defendant were married in Russia. At the time, the defendant's parents were petitioning to leave Russia to go to Israel. [Rita] promised Yakov's family before she married Yakov that if her parents left Russia, she would stay with her new husband, [yet] she broke that promise. When her parents [three months after Rita and Yakov had married] received permission to leave, she left Russia to go with them to Israel. For three months the defendant did not contact her husband. Then she realized she was pregnant and she campaigned to get him out of Russia."

"She is a resourceful woman and she was ultimately successful in getting Yakov out of Russia. And what's the first thing that happens when they are together in Israel? They fight," said Daly.

The prosecutor reminded the jury of statements in the record attesting to Rita's condecension toward Yakov: the young scientist "had just settled into a research position in microbiology at the Weizmann Institute . . . when the defendant told him that he was not a success and that he should quit because he would make more money as a furniture maker!" Michael Gluzman's recollections of his brother's early years in Israel were coming back to haunt Rita. Reminding the jury of Yakov's eventual preeminence as a pioneer cancer researcher, Deirdre Daly continued with comments on Rita Gluzman's cruelty toward her husband over the years, particularly after the couple had moved to the U.S. in 1977.

Lest the jury had forgotten the financial importance of Yakov Gluzman to Rita's existence both personally and professionally, Daly continued: "Yakov [in 1996] is making substantially more than the defendant. It is

Yakov who is paying for the big house and nice lifestyle.
It is Yakov's money that's being injected into ECI in
1993 and again in 1994 to keep the company going."
Daly reviewed the financial data of Yakov's settlement
offer to Rita as proof of not only his earning veracity,
but of Rita's need for even more than the nearly-
$800,000 offer. She also needed control of ECI, which
had slowed the progress of the couple's divorce action.
Nobody within the jury box had ever seen $800,000
before, and, it would be learned later, could not understand why Rita hadn't accepted Yakov's generous offer.

But it was Rita's obssessive behavior that Daly was
presenting to the jury; her anger at losing her husband,
even if she had little romantic feeling for the popular
Yasha thirty years into their relationship. And Rita's
need for control, most significantly of ECI and its books,
was further proof of her nature. "Why is ECI so
important to Rita Gluzman? It was ... her company,
she ran it, she told the employees what to do, it was her
life," Daly reminded the jury. "ECI also supported her
lifestyle ... it paid for her BMW, the cable TV in her
house, the apartment in Fair Lawn where Zelenin lived.
The company even paid her mortgage for two months
in 1995. It hired her son, her sister, and her cousin
Zelenin and paid for cars, all of them—three different
Ford Tauruses and a Miata."

By the time Yakov withdrew his settlement offer in
late 1995, Daly continued, "Rita never knew if she would
get as generous an offer again." Yakov had threatened
to deadlock ECI if Rita continued to withhold the company's books from its largest shareholder, its benefactor,
and "that would have stripped Rita Gluzman of control,
and she panicked at the thought of losing ECI."

In late 1995, Rita had told her friend Gary Schnayderman that "we cannot let Yakov take the business away,"

a sentiment she had, to her regret, also shared with Zelenin.

Daly reviewed Rita's expenses as she had claimed in her divorce response to Yakov: it took $132,000 a year to keep her afloat, including the clothing allowance of $1,000 a month, and her physical therapy and counseling, which came to nearly $1,400 monthly, according to Rita. Members of the jury had tried not to blanch during the reiteration of the widow Gluzman's expensive lifestyle. Daly reminded them that on Rita's draw from ECI of $50,000 a year, the shortfall had to be made up somewhere. It fell on Yakov Gluzman to subsidize that shortfall, which he had almost uncomplainingly done.

But the heart of the money issue was in ECI's continued subsidy from Yakov. He had established the company by loaning it $300,000, and six years later it was a break-even proposition, despite having grown to $3 million in sales annually. Rita's expense policy accounted for ECI's inability to show a solid profit. Her $50,000 draw was not an issue, considering the work she did as ECI's chief executive. And somebody would have had to do the work her mother, sister, and Zelenin did. Ilan was capable of working at any number of large electronics companies. But ECI subsidized Rita on expenses other start-up companies would hardly have considered "ordinary," such as her hairdresser, personal trainer, clothing, and other personal items, which had put a serious dent in the company's margins. The person most interested in ECI showing a profit had been Yakov Gluzman, its financier, who was denied access to the company's books. He was about to withdraw his subsidy, and about to effectively disband the corporation, in the divorce action. This, Daly stated, petrified

Rita and forced her hand as to whether or not she should kill her husband.

When Rita had found out about Yakov sending money home to Israel, to his brother and to Chaim Gluzman, she became enraged, and had sprung the extortion plot. The money Yasha had sent abroad, $150,000, was money Rita knew she wouldn't see; the extortionist had demanded that sum in order that Yakov's affair with Raisa Korenblit not be exposed. The coincidence was not to be believed.

Deirdre Daly reminded the jurors of Rita's anger at discovering Yakov's relationship with Raisa. Opening her husband's mail and finding the letter from Bill Bradley to Yakov and learning in May 1995 of Yakov's attempts to win a visa for the Israeli had startled Rita, setting her on a course to disturb Yakov's plans, and to harm this new rival for her husband's affection. Simply knowing that her husband wished to separate from her hadn't upset Rita as much as knowing of the existence of another woman, even after twenty six years together and at the end of that relationship. Rita Gluzman was determined to retain not only as much money as she could from her union with Yakov, but had decided to unravel any plans her husband might have had to begin life anew.

Finally, Daly told the jury again of the insurance policies and Rita's likely collection of the many hundreds of thousands of dollars Yakov's insurers would have paid his widow, regardless of the conclusiveness of Yakov's death. This again served in the prosecution's mind to debunk the defense argument that because of the length of time involved in collecting death benefits on a person deemed missing, rather than known to be dead, Rita would have had little motive to dispose of

Yakov's body parts. And, she hadn't known Yakov had changed his beneficiary from his wife to his son, Ilan.

Daly itemized the death benefits: from New York Life, $350,000. From TIAA/CREF, $213,000. From American Home Products, $170,000. From Lederle, $230,000 and another policy specifying death and dismemberment, which would kick in $250,000. Yakov Gluzman had been insured to the hilt, and Rita had known it.

However, Daly told the jury, "That amount doesn't even include the assets she would receive after his death. The grand total of the policies is $1.3 million. That money in and of itself gave Rita Gluzman, a woman who was obsessed with money, a motive to kill her husband. And what does she say in the court papers?" the U.S. Attorney continued, referring to the divorce court. "That the court compel Yakov not to change the beneficiaries of any of his life insurance policies. So that if anything happens to Yakov Gluzman, Rita Gluzman will be the first in line to collect on those policies!" Daly had reinforced the "greed" motive and Rita's very solid opportunity to control the destiny of Yakov's insurance policies.

"Now," Daly concluded, "the defendant has suggested and may argue that this is not a motive for her to kill her husband because the plot here was to have the body disappear. And thus, Rita Gluzman would not have been able to collect the insurance. That's simply not true.

"You heard the testimony of four different insurance representatives. And they all said that in cases where bodies are not found, beneficiaries can go to court, and get a finding that the person is in fact dead although no body has been found. The time period in New Jersey [may] be five years, but those time periods are not set in stone, and if a court can find based on the circumstances relating to the disappearance of the insured that there is enough to show that the insured is dead, then the beneficiary can collect," Daly continued.

"And in this case, there was signficant evidence to show that Yakov would have been, had been killed. No one would have seen him—his family, his friends, his employees. And there was blood found in his apartment. So the defendant would have been able to collect this money if she'd gotten away with this murder!"

Deirdre Daly was reaching her stride in the prosecutorial summation. She'd slowly built on matters of court record attesting to Rita's motives and had demonstrated the big payoff that awaited Yakov Gluzman's widow if she had successfully disposed of her husband's body. Now, Daly reminded the jurors of the extortion charges, crucial to linking all the elements of U.S. v. Gluzman.

"What is Rita doing in the fall of 1995? While her husband is trying to get her to agree to a divorce settlement? On September 12, she flies to Germany, and on to Israel. Her husband is also in Israel, but they don't travel together. Michael Gluzman testified that he picked up Yakov at the airport and Rita was not with him. Yakov visits his family and looks into the possibility of opening up a business. What does Rita Gluzman do? She meets with David Rom, the investigator you saw in the videotape from Israel. She meets Rom, pays him a thousand dollars cash, gives him information about Raisa Korenblit, and a list of questions she wants answers to. She asks Rom to verify, bring her proof of the relationship between Yakov and Rita. It's obvious that when you ask an investigator for proof of a relationship, he understands that what he is supposed to do is get photographs.

"Now, why does Rita want those photographs? She already had proof of the relationship. Yakov hadn't even filed for divorce yet. And adultery isn't relevant in a no-fault divorce state like New Jersey. She wanted the photographs for the extortion letters.''

Daly reviewed Rita's relationship with Rom, how Rom had retained Benny Lefkowitz to do the surveillance of Yakov and Raisa, and Rita's urgency in getting the photos to her in the U.S. as soon as possible in fall 1995. And what do you know, Daly continued the extortion letters to Yakov's father Chaim, intercepted by Michael Gluzman to prevent a heart attack in the elder Mr. Gluzman, had arrived beginning in October 1995, conveniently just weeks after Rom had FedExed—with ECI's account—his photos of Raisa and Yakov together to Rita Gluzman.

Deirdre Daly's summation would last for two hours, her itemization of the government's evidence and witness testimony in the case of U.S. v. Rita Gluzman meticulously organized and recited. Because the law dictates precise use of the record, only that entered into the court's daily entries throughout the trial may be referred to at summation. The Ivy League prosecutor had not been appointed chief of the U.S. Attorney's office in White Plains for being less than thorough, and reading every piece of condemning evidence back to the jury was necessary to remind the twelve individuals of what they'd heard the past three weeks.

The extortion case appeared solid, and Daly reminded the jury of David Rom and Benny Lefkowitz's photos, which they'd sent to Rita, ending up as part of the threatening letters to Chaim Gluzman. That when the extortionist had said Yakov's and Raisa's relationship would be "exposed," that everybody had already known of the affair in Israel anyway, at least those who mattered. With the coincidental amounts demanded—$100,000 first and $50,000 added on later—compared with the amounts Rita and Yakov had disputed in the fall of 1995, it appeared to all as though nobody but Rita could have been the extortionist.

Reminding the jurors of Rita's attempts to hire both Joe Mullen and Bob Burton and Rita's obsession with "preserving an American family" must have made Rita Gluzman squirm in her chair at the defense table as her strange conversations—and the recruitment of the private investigator and the bounty hunter to prevent Korenblit's union with Yakov—were replayed for all. Pre-empting the defense's contention that somehow the investigator and his electronic "sweeper," Mike Rizzuto, had tried to shake Rita down, Daly reminded the jury that no one other than Rita Gluzman had benefitted from Yakov's death, and that Rizzuto and Mullen had quickly disassociated themselves from the hysterical woman, having sensed something wrong in the behavior of their erstwhile client.

But the biggest portion of Deirdre Daly's lengthy and meticulous summation was reserved for Vladimir Zelenin's testimony, which the defense had tried unsuccessfully to impeach. Recalling the frightening statements the Russian had made during his three and half days on the witness stand, Daly used the accomplice's detailed recollection of the murder of Yakov Gluzman to clinch the case against Rita Gluzman.

Fortunately for Rita, this wasn't totalitarian Russia, where the prosecutor's summation would conclude and she would be ushered off for execution. Hochheiser and Rosen still had a chance to influence the twelve jurors about their client's non-involvement in the murder. The attorneys had run out of technical challenges to Rita's prosecution, and may have already been looking to the appellate courts as they organized a rebuttal to Daly's damning summation.

"That was a pretty scary summation by Deirdre Daly," Hochheiser opened to the jury, giving a fair preview of the defense's last great effort to instill some reasonable doubt as to Rita's guilt. "It was in the finest tradition of the Office of the United States Attorney for the Southern District.

"First, the reason that Deirdre Daly's summation is so powerful is because it really homogenizes all the evidence," Hochheiser continued. "It's kind of like equal opportunity summation. Every piece of evidence is just as good as every other piece of evidence, and it's all part of the story, like you tell the story of the three little pigs. It's not like 'maybe' this happened, 'maybe' that happened, it goes on from beginning to end, and it's everything that the government has, as a theory, woven into ultimate conclusion, which [Daly] says are facts that are proved. Now, everybody kind of knew what the government's theory is and what the facts are, that they would claim to prove. Miss Daly's summation would be valid if two things: one, if after we evaluate the quality of the evidence and the process here, we find that it's reliable. Then such a summation does in fact characterize the facts in the case. And if what she says is true, then everybody she speaks about is guilty of everything she speaks about."

Hochheiser's remarks were intended to warm up to the jury; but in fact, their mixed message served only to confuse all listeners. It was a valiant stretch by the defender, though he seemed on the verge of accusing the U.S. Attorney of malicious prosecution or of framing his client.

"And so you might be asking yourself," Hochheiser continued, "well, what's your job? What is your job if Deirdre Daly's summation is really as powerful and as valid as it might sound? Your job is to look at the evidence underlying that summation, to look at the evidence in this case.

"First of all, Miss Daly told you that—you can tell how good the summation is because I keep mentioning her name," Hochheiser stumbled, interrupting himself. "It stings me," the attorney went on. "But she told you that, when I get up, what you are going to hear after her facts, you are going to hear smoke screens. You are going to hear my spin. And she didn't use the word, but basically she told you to be on the alert, because I'm gonna, I am gonna really be giving you a fake rendition of the evidence." Hochheiser paused. "And I can assure you that's not going to happen. And if it does happen, you can just disregard what I say and turn me off, so I'm going to be pretty careful to make that not happen."

Five minutes into his closing arguments on behalf of Rita Gluzman, Larry Hochheiser was trying to reestablish rapport with the jury he'd faced up close for three weeks. Hochheiser's professionalism enabled him to regroup, somewhat, to try to persuade the jury to ignore Deirdre Daly's crafted, unimpeachable presentation of Rita Gluzman's criminal acts.

"Now, we can take a method here and we can look at this chronologically. We can look at the crimes. We could look at the witnesses. We could look at the concepts. And probably what's going to happen is we are going to do a little bit of each," Hochheiser continued, "and we are gonna have a little bit of maybe free association, because concepts run into witnesses and witnesses run into concepts and crime.

"Now, if you want to talk about smoke and mirrors, all right. I made a note because it reminded me of something I did as a demonstration for law school class once. And Miss Daly said that this was a piece of logic.

"Vladimir Zelenin said that Rita wore gloves and cleaned up very well. And the proof that that's true is that there's no evidence that Rita Gluzman—no forensic evidence—committed this crime to be found in the apartment, and the blood is all cleaned up.

"That was like when I had this assignment to give a summation for a hypothetical case of a drug kingpin, and there just wasn't any evidence against the drug kingpin in this hypothetical class presentation. I fashioned this fairly clever argument at the time, that a definition of a drug kingpin was a person who insulated himself from the rest of the people who are working for him, made it so there wouldn't be any evidence to be found against him, and positioned himself in such a way that people wouldn't know what he was doing and be able to talk about it. Then I argued, you see, we have proved this guy is a drug kingpin because all of these things are true. There is no evidence against him. He doesn't seem to be connected. Et cetera, et cetera. So I caution you in the beginning about this kind of circular logic concerning finding a human being guilty of a crime that Vladimir Zelenin told you carries a life sentence."

In most circles, Hochheiser's argument would appear specious, begging the question as it does in its comparison to a gangland defense and defense posturing compared to an act of domestic violence such as Rita's.

"Now let me start where we started the other day," Hochheiser resumed. "Okay, if Rita Gluzman is innocent, then what does the trial of an innocent person look like? Remember I raised that before. And this seems like it's a facetious, silly point, but it's not at all, because we come to think of what a trial looks like of a guilty person. Okay. People say the words of guilt, and if they are true the person is guilty. What is the trial of an innocent person like?

"I was watching *Matlock* the other day—and I apologize for that—and on television, in a trial of an innocent person, [it] looks like a witness [is] on stand, and the lawyer gets right up here [at the witness box] and [in] examining the witness and saying to the witness whatever the heck she's saying to the witness, the judge doesn't say, 'Get back to the podium,' or anything like that. And the witness's mascara starts to run down her face because she's guilty, she's really the guilty person, and the defendant is innocent.

"In *Perry Mason*—I am showing my age—there was always a guilty person out in the audience who would stand up and say, 'I did it', in front of a judge and a court reporter. You know, like maybe Vladimir there.

"Isn't that interesting? We talk about this as a search for truth, and nobody wants to win, and nobody cares about winning. I mean, we are going to get into some of these details, but isn't it interesting? I have tried to put myself into that position. My father is convicted of murdering a person and cutting them up into sixty-seven pieces. Okay. He makes a deal with the government and testifies against Rita Gluzman, and I come to court to hear summations and to see the verdict. Now is there really an interest that the Zelenins have in the process of this case, in the verdict of this case?"

Hochheiser once again plowed into the prosecution's chief witness, trying as he and Rosen had during the trial to sully the Russian's testimony, to suggest that the government had made a sweetheart deal with the admitted killer in order to put Rita Gluzman away. There was no conspiracy on the part of the police department to persecute and incarcerate innocent Jewish émigrés from the Ukraine, of course, but Rita's attorneys were pulling no punches in trying to impugn her cousin.

"Now, the government probably forgot to mention the argument concerning the deal that Vladimir made, but do we really believe what you are asked to believe? And that is, that Vladimir Zelenin really has no interest in what your verdict is in this case, and his son has no interest, and that everything is all going to be the same. Except 'trust us,' because you're never gonna see what Vladimir Zelenin gets. Okay . . . Well, of course, you know," Hochheiser continued, "you could say, nobody is sure what Sammy the Bull [Gravano] was going to get, either."

Hochheiser finished his Matlock comparison, telling the jury that "the trial of an innocent person looks the same as the trial of a guilty person. The difference is a question of quality, of cohesion, of motives and benefits. The difference is a question of reliability of the evidence that you hear."

Larry Hochheiser thought he had found two or three sympathetic faces in the jury box. One would be enough to have a hung jury. Two or three would be enough to throw off the prosecution's months of work and Zelenin's testimony completely. After reviewing for the jurors the meaning of trial by jury, and the standards to which the prosecution is held in proving guilt, Hochheiser threw himself back into the hypothetical.

"Is there anyone here that really has any doubt that in this country, in this building, in this courtroom, in other courtrooms in this building, all over, every day, that innocent people get charged with serious crimes, including murder, and go to trial? Innocent people. And it's not easy, okay. They don't look innocent. They look guilty. Because if they looked innocent they wouldn't be here, there wouldn't be any problem at all."

"Without Vladimir Zelenin, there is no case against Rita Gluzman. Think about it," Hochheiser continued. "Everything else is so-called corroboration. I am going to explain to you why that appears to be corroboration but is not corroboration. You may be looking at me and saying, how are you going to do that? I am going to show it to you, and you are going to understand it, I believe, when I get finished talking to you.

"The government made a deal with the devil, so to speak, and they don't call it a deal, because that has a negative ring to it. But it is a deal. They call it a cooperation agreement. They elevate it. They tell you, 'Oh, we despise Vladimir Zelenin just as you do.' But they enter into what they call a 'cooperation agreement' and a negotiated deal with the public defenders for Vladimir Zelenin. And what is the deal?" After a lengthy explanation about the tenets of an agreement, Hochheiser still could not place any benefit to Zelenin other than his *not* being executed, which couldn't happen anyway once he'd pled guilty. His comparison of Zelenin to Sammy "The Bull" Gravano had fallen flat, as the parallels between the two men, one a mob turncoat whose testimony had convicted an underworld leader, the other a poor immigrant who was helping to prosecute Rita Gluzman, was brave but an overreach. Nobody believed that Zelenin would receive a light sentence or be let free or sign book contracts and be put into the Witness Protection Program, after leaving the Quarropas courthouse. Even if Zelenin's sentence had been reduced to fifteen years, as Hochheiser had suggested at sidebar to Parker and Daly, what incentive would that have provided the government's star witness?

Hochheiser argued that Zelenin's sentence should

occur as soon as possible, so that the jury would have the chance to see how lenient the court would be. But Parker deemed it a moot point.

So Hochheiser reviewed the other benefits to Vladimir Zelenin from his cooperation with the U.S. Attorney: no deportation; a stay in a federal prison, as opposed to a gloomy state prison; access to his sons. Not exactly a lottery windfall. Then the lawyer repeated from the record Zelenin's admitted misstatements about his wife's death, his application for political asylum, and other less than honest practices the Russian had employed as a matter of survival. "He is a perjurer! He is a man who made a deal. He is a murderer. He is a psychopath, a monster. He cut up the body of a man who was a friend and benefactor, a man who helped him! Unlike Mr. Valvo's jurisdiction, in the federal jurisdiction you don't need corroboration for a jury to convict Rita Gluzman on the testimony of a monster like this, of an accomplice in a crime, of a man who made a deal. The judge gave you instructions that you have to receive his testimony with special care and caution, but there is no protection in this jurisdiction that says you need corroboration. That's why a person like this is so dangerous."

The jury's estimation of Vladimir Zelenin had not changed since the day of his introduction to them the week before. He appeared to be a disturbed, cold-blooded murderer who had been forced into killing Yakov Gluzman, was happy to be alive at this point and miserable over having killed the one person who had actually been kind to him during his few years in the United States.

Hochheiser tried to downplay Rita's material enjoyment, first by telling the jury that her BMW "is not a luxurious limo. It's a Five Series, which the government well knows is taken by the certified public accountant as eighty percent for business."

Nobody on the jury had a BMW in the Five Series for which he or she received a tax deduction.

Hochheiser continued his assault on the government's financial data used by the prosecutors to demonstrate Rita's expensive habits. He tried to lessen the damaging aspects of ECI's profit-and-loss chart, which showed minor losses over the previous few years. Hochheiser tried to point out how fortunate Zelenin was, compared to other immigrants without papers, in making $8 an hour working for ECI. A number of the defender's points made good sense. Rita's having used ECI to pay some of her ordinary bills hadn't placed her in the arena of big-time swindlers who had ruthlessly looted their companies. In the realm of modern-day America, Rita Gluzman was just getting by, paying the mortgage, going to the gym, having a haircut.

But the prosecution's contention had been that Yakov Gluzman was paying for her indulgences, and his sponsorship was coming to an end.

Hochheiser took a break an hour into his summation, telling Judge Parker that he might need more time for his closing remarks. The judge, empathetic with the weary defense lawyer who had spent many a sleepless night trying to find anything he could to acquit Rita Gluzman, called a brief recess.

Hochheiser resumed his defense of Rita shortly after. He reopened his address to the jury almost resignedly. "I guess it's painfully obvious that I'm sensitive to the fact that I realize as a matter of fact, if not as a matter of law, that prosecutors tend to have more credibility than defense attorneys. I mean, that's just a fact of the matter. I guess when I was a prosecutor, I had more credibility than when I was a defense lawyer. These are the times we live in. So, I'm constantly saying to you, don't take my word for it because I work for Rita Gluzman. And I try to overcome that by doing just the opposite of what Miss Daly suggested and not putting spins on things, but reading things there can be no argument about." Hochheiser's folksy *Matlock* approach stirred the jury briefly.

"Now I told you that the government's theory about insurance is not only all wet, but it's illogical and it's convoluted," Hochheiser continued. "They are trying to tell you that one of the motives here is money, the big motive here is money, and that insurance is the big portion of the money, and [they] keep talking about the fact if people disappear . . ." Hochheiser cut himself off and proceeded to review Zelenin's conversation with Rita on direct examination, concerning the insurance policies on Yakov's life and the result if Yakov were to disappear. Oddly, the defense lawyer acknowledged that his client and the prosecution's witness had discussed the ramifications of killing Yakov and how it would be difficult to collect insurance money on a missing person, and how seemingly Zelenin had dissuaded Rita from expecting insurance. It was a strange interjection meant to clear Rita Gluzman of an insurance motive, but lending credibility to Zelenin.

From their perch at the prosecution's table, Deirdre Daly, Cathy Seibel, and Lou Valvo were watching Hochheiser try valiantly to disprove their case. They hadn't interrupted the defense attorney, and the three waited for the revelation of reasonable doubt the veteran lawyer needed to impart on the jury.

Hochheiser continued his rebuttal of the prosecution's summation throughout the afternoon of the 28th. He tried to show that the CVS clerk, Huffman, had been steered into identifying Rita by Hilda Kogut, the nineteen-year veteran of the FBI who did not have a single complaint on her work record. He tried to show how the wiretappers were somehow dishonest, were trying to shake Rita down. He tried again to show how Zelenin was a monster, in case the jurors had forgotten just how gruesome the Russian's act had been. Hochheiser was trying to counter each piece of government evidence against his client. But the Rockland District Attorney's Office alone had collected more than 500 exhibits, and it would have taken a conspiracy beyond belief for all those involved in the investigation of Yakov Gluzman's death to have set Rita up. Hochheiser had acquitted clients who had been caught in the act with eyewitnesses and fingerprints on the murder weapon in his career. But deconstructing the case against Rita Gluzman was a tough challenge. There had to be something left, some challenge to the government's case, something that would get the doubtful juror in the box to reject the prosecution's case.

But there was nothing left. Judge Parker adjourned the courtroom for the day, and granted Hochheiser's wish to finish his defense in the morning. Stranger things had happened in the law during the twentieth century than a defense lawyer finding the necessary argument at the close of a trial on a good night's sleep. As Rita was made ready for the ride to her quarters at Valhalla, Hochheiser and Rosen searched for their final words.

The next day Larry Hochheiser arrived at Quarropas refreshed and with an argument to rekindle his summation of Rita's innocence. The prosecution's biggest direct link of Rita's participation, other than Zelenin's testimony, was Rita's purchase of the bandages Easter morning at CVS. The clerk, Leonard Huffman, had been caught up in a murder investigation quite by accident. Hochheiser tore into the young man's statements again. How could he remember Rita Gluzman, unaided? How much influence did Hilda Kogut's showing the clerk Rita's picture have on his recall? Hochheiser derided the government's use of Huffman's memory as "pseudo-corroboration" or "reverse corroboration." The prosecutors were "backing into" corroboration. The attorney was doing his best to instill doubt, invoking the pertinent historical analogy to William Randolph Hearst telling his reporters in Cuba, "You provide the headlines, and I'll provide the war!" to suggest the DA and U.S. Attorney had instructed the detectives and FBI to do the same with regard to Rita.

The unstated difficulty Larry Hochheiser faced with the jury, however, was in showing the men and women who held his client's life in the balance how the prosecutors, with a confessed killer in their custody, sought to chase Rita when they could have simply closed their case with Zelenin who had already pleaded guilty to the crime.

But Hochheiser was getting a second wind, the competitor in him for the jury's hearts and minds returning, conceding nothing to Deirdre Daly's summation or to Cathy Seibel's and Lou Valvo's two-week hammering of the witnesses who had contributed to the look of culpability on Rita's face. The lawyer reconstructed Easter morning, in an effort to show why Rita could not have accompanied Zelenin, why the trip from East Rutherford to Upper Saddle River was impossible, how Ilan's failure to have a watch and therefore not remember exactly when he saw his mother proved she could have been at home all along. Then the changes in Zelenin's statements to Sgt. Tom Goldrick, how the government had somehow steered the confessed accomplice into implicating Rita and coaching an exact timeline to the witness, overwhelmed by the language barrier and intimidated by the police into telling them whatever they wanted to know about Rita Gluzman.

Judge Parker interrupted Hochheiser, asking for a sidebar. The defense had taken nearly five hours over two days to present its summation, and Parker wanted to know how much longer Rita's attorney needed. "It's getting very repetitive," the judge admonished. "What are your plans?"

"I have to do the extortion and the flight," Hochheiser told Parker and Daly at the bench.

Parker was impatient. "You said less than an hour [Tuesday] and it's already been an hour and forty minutes."

Hochheiser's exhaustion was showing. "I don't think I'm repeating much at all. I'll move it right along and get finished with it. The extortion and flight is pretty quick.

"It's a tough case. I never gave this summation before. I'm doing it as quick as I can. It's not like I'm reading something that I wrote."

Hochheiser agreed to finish within the hour, as Parker called a recess to give the jury a break. When the attorneys resumed, Hochheiser called into question Bob Burton's statements, and the finding by Rodriguez and the Bergen detectives of the bounty hunter's card in the air duct behind Rita's clothes dryer. Then Hochheiser touched a nerve in the prosecutors that showed he'd pulled out all the stops. He invoked Ilan Gluzman.

"I think his testimony about sleeping on the side of the road for the long trip from Staten Island into New Jersey was fascinating. Someday I would like to learn more about that, and I would really like to know why he was so evasive about an ax that he knew belonged in the garage and was there all the time," said Hochheiser.

Deirdre Daly flinched, angry at the pain Ilan Gluzman was made to endure, first at having lost his father so brutally, his mother on trial for the crime, and the young man now questioned about his whereabouts again. The prosecutor thought the defense attorney had no shame to suggest that Ilan somehow was connected to the crime.

Hochheiser tried vainly to prove that Rita had not been the author or instigator of the extortion letters to Chaim Gluzman, but David Rom's video was a lot to overcome. It was likewise with Rita's flight issue, but those matters seemed small in comparison to the larger crime. Then the lawyer wrapped it up. The court broke for lunch, with Daly's rebuttal summation to begin after the jury returned.

Daly began with sympathy for the jury's endurance in listening to the long arguments in the case, and acknowledged the prosecution's job. "I'm speaking a second time because the burden is on the government. The burden is to prove this case beyond a reasonable doubt. If the government's job were to prove this defendant innocent, as Mr. Hochheiser says, we wouldn't be here. We could not prove her innocent.

"There is overwhelming evidence that this woman was desperate. She taped her husband, she extorted her husband, and she killed her husband. That's why we're here.

"The defense would have you believe that within an eight-month period, from September 1995, when the wiretapping and extortion occurred, through April 1996, when Yakov Gluzman was killed, that six people, most of whom didn't know Yakov Gluzman, most of whom came from different parts of the world, decided to terrorize and kill Yakov Gluzman. Mr. Hochheiser would have you believe that Mike Rizzuto and Ed Mateo, the guys from Queens, decided to wiretap Yakov Gluzman; that David Rom and Benny Levkowitz decided to extort Yakov Gluzman; and, finally, that some other unknown person got together with Vladimir Zelenin to kill Yakov Gluzman. Mr. Hochheiser suggested today that perhaps it was Igor, Zelenin's son, or perhaps Ilan, Yakov's own son.

"Ladies and gentlemen, do you think that Igor or Ilan look like the woman the Smiths described to you? Do you think that Igor or Ilan look like the woman who bought the bandages from Lenny Huffman? Do you think that Igor or Ilan sound like the woman on the tapes with Zelenin plotting the murder?" Daly had been infuriated at Hochheiser's suggestion of either of the boys' involvement.

"Where were Igor and Ilan after the murder? Cooperating with the police. They weren't hiding out in Cold Spring Harbor," Daly continued.

Reiterating Rita's activities in fall 1995: flying to Israel, hiring Rom, then hiring Rizzuto and Mateo to bug the Pearl River apartment, Daly debunked the defense's conspiracy argument. The U.S. Attorney reviewed, the salient evidence: Rita's trip to LaGuardia Easter afternoon and Rom's tapes, and got to the root of the defense claim. "If you believe the government is trying to frame this defendant, you should go right into that jury room and come right back out and acquit. There is no evidence in the record of this. And if the government wanted to frame this defendant, why didn't they just put a fingerprint on one of the murder weapons? It's an absurd argument and a desperate argument to distract you from the facts and the evidence in this case!

"What else is there to corroborate Vladimir Zelenin? Her [Rita Gluzman] fingerprint in the car with the body parts."

Daly reviewed Goldrick's testimony of Zelenin's statements the day of the crime, once again reminding the jurors of the premeditation the Bergen detective had uncovered as Zelenin started to loosen up under questioning,

"Hochheiser also argued that Zelenin swore at the defendant when he left the witness stand. You can imagine the hostility and anger running between these two people.

"Zelenin will spend at least twenty years, perhaps the rest of his life, in jail for this horrendous crime, and it was all the defendant's idea. She set it in motion. She recruited him. You can imagine the anger he must feel toward her.

"You should not acquit this defendant because you are disgusted by Zelenin or because you are concerned that he will not be punished severely enough. He has pled guilty to murder in two different courts, in state court and before Judge Parker. Despite Larry Hochheiser's suggestion, Zelenin knows that he faces twenty years," the prosecutor continued. The minimum sentence was a part of the court record, and Daly reminded the jury that the Russian would be doing twenty years of hard time at the very least, even with his cooperation with the government.

Once again debunking the defense conspiracy story, Daly reminded the jury of Zelenin's dependency on his cousin and how it would have been foolish for him to have framed Rita. All support woud have vanished.

Daly had reserved some of her disgust with the defense summation for her next argument.

"If there is any question in your mind how cold-blooded this defendant is, think about Ilan. She abandoned him after she murdered his father. He had to take care of everything alone. And what did she do in court right in front of you? The defense has suggested that Ilan killed his own father. You remember the questions? 'Where were you on the night of the murder? Oh, so you fell asleep on the side of the road.' The nasty letter he wrote a few years ago to his father. 'Ilan, you refused to take a lie detector test, didn't you?'

"They tried to implicate Ilan in this murder! And of course you learned that the reason Ilan was asked to take a lie detector test is because the police could not believe that his mother would have abandoned him and fled without keeping in contact with him. He was never a suspect in this case, because there is no evidence linking him to this murder!

"What does this show? This shows how desperate this defendant is to distract you from the evidence in this case. It's absurd and it's unspeakable that she would do that to her own son."

Finally, Deirdre Daly turned Hochheiser's summation homily against the defender. "What does the trial of an innocent person look like? It looks like a trial where a woman attends her husband's funeral, consoles her son when she learns her husband has been brutally murdered, not a woman who flees, hides out in Cold Spring Harbor using aliases, stealing license plates, calling airlines, reading travel books, calling people asking them for cash and false identification. This is a trial of a guilty person plotting her escape.

"Imagine Rita Gluzman's anger at the thought that Yakov Gluzman was leaving her. This is the man who she fought for and got out of Russia. This is the man she thought was no longer good in bed. This man was leaving her for another woman. She was furious. She was enraged. What corroborates Vladimir Zelenin?

"The Henckel knife, the murder weapon, this defendant's choice of knife. You heard that again and again. The tapes. They are plotting the murder.

"The timing. No one else knew who had been cut up so brutally, murdered, at three on Sunday other than Sergeant Goldrick, Zelenin, and this defendant. How did she know? Because she was one of the killers, and at that time she was at the airport.

"Who is the one who benefits, the one who would benefit from this murder if they got away with it? Rita Gluzman, [by] millions of dollars!

"And who is the one that's angry at Yakov Gluzman, the only one in the world who wanted him dead? The defendant. She had a fair trial, and remember, she was present when Zelenin cut up her husband's body. She is responsible for this nightmare that has shattered so many lives.

"Yakov Gluzman is also entitled to a fair trial. The government asks only that you do what justice demands, that you convict this defendant on all counts for the cruel murder of her husband. Thank you."

The prosecutor's summation and rebuttal left little to the jury's imagination. Shortly before one, Judge Parker excused the jury to the conference room where they would conduct their deliberations. Throughout the afternoon, the forewoman requested certain details— the medical examiner's report, the phone records, some other details from the record, but by 5:30 P.M., four hours after they'd entered deliberations, the jury had yet to reach a verdict. Parker excused the men and women with admonishments to put their statements on hold until the following morning, and meet in the jury room to continue. The prosecutors and defense lawyers would have to wait yet another day for the case's climax. Rita would return to Valhalla.

The Verdict

Larry Hochheiser and Mike Rosen got to the Quarropas courthouse early on Wednesday morning. Reporters and family members jammed the fifth-floor courtroom, anxious to know of Rita Gluzman's fate. Numerous colleagues from Lederle sat quietly in the back of the courtroom. Four weeks of a contentious trial had left little doubt in observers' minds as to the veracity of the government's case, given Zelenin's four days of testimony and Rita's apparently clear motive to have wanted Yakov dead. The prosecution's case had seemed so efficient, succinct, linear, that some wondered why it had taken the better part of Tuesday afternoon for the jurors to deliberate, then be excused overnight to continue deciding Rita's fate the next day. Nothing could be certain when left in the hands of twelve jurors, especially since there wasn't the absolute proof Rita Gluzman had been at the Pearl River apartment when Yakov was killed, only convincing logic that she had indeed participated with Zelenin.

Both Hochheiser and Rosen had analyzed the jury over and over in the three weeks since the trial had begun, wondering which of the men and women would be likely to be sympathetic to Rita or, better, hostile to the government. The lawyers had counted at least three skeptics, or so they had guessed, jurors who may have given Rita the benefit of some doubt. With fingers crossed, they comforted Rita as Judge Parker entered from his chambers.

"Have you reached a verdict?" Parker asked the woman who had been picked to lead the jury.

"We have, Your Honor," came her reply.

After the forewoman's response, a quiet came over the courtroom as the bailiff kept an eye on all assembled, including the large gallery of Yakov Gluzman's friends, family, and co-workers. There was rarely certainty in predicting a jury's verdict.

Rita had been found guilty on all but the extortion charge. Conspiracy to commit murder: guilty. Interstate domestic violence resulting in death: guilty. Illegal interception of oral communications: guilty. Use of a device to intercept oral communications: guilty.

It was no consolation that the jurors hadn't convicted on the extortion charge, but they simply weren't convinced beyond all doubt by the statements from David Rom and Benny Lefkowitz that Rita was behind the shakedown of Chaim Gluzman, and the extortion charge was by now a moot point. The most serious of the U.S. Attorney's indictments and the most novel charge against Rita had been accepted by twelve men and women: that Rita Gluzman had crossed state lines to commit an act of domestic violence that resulted in her husband Yakov Gluzman's death. They had believed

Vladimir Zelenin after all, and the jury had had little problem with the corroborative evidence outlined by Daly, Seibel, and Valvo. Rita's head fell into her hands while Mike Rosen and Larry Hochheiser tried to comfort her.

The prosecution table was happily abuzz. Valvo congratulated Cathy Seibel, then Deirdre Daly, and the two U.S. Attorneys returned the compliment to the unofficial team leader of the prosecution's search for justice. Tom Goldrick, Jake Szpicek, Steve Colantonio, and Tom Hoffmann came forward from the spectators' gallery to congratulate the prosecutors. Their months of meticulous work and reconstruction of the crime had paid off, and there was no uncertainty as to the result.

Over in New City, Mike Bongiorno waited for Lou Valvo's telephone call.

After recording the verdicts, Judge Parker instructed the clerk to set sentencing for May 1. This would allow the judge three months to decide Rita's fate. Federal sentencing guidelines are unambiguous for a crime such as hers, and few expected Rita to ever see the outside world again.

In the first section of the spectator seats, Ilan Gluzman was uneasy, but looked resigned to his mother's fate. Ilan had been put into the most difficult of all positions. He had lost his father in a manner too sickening to imagine. The warm, bright man who had inspired Ilan into a career in technology and provided a comfortable life for his young son was gone forever. Now Ilan had lost his mother, too. Ilan had guaranteed Rosen and Hochheiser's fees with proceeds from his father's insurance policies, a biting irony but one the conscientious son had dealt with. Ilan also had lost nine months of his life bearing witness to the investigation and trial while he tried to sustain ECI.

On May 1, at Rita's sentencing, Judge Parker received the victim's impact statements. Ilan chose not to speak directly to the court, though he sent a letter to Parker requesting leniency for his mother. Chaim and Sophia Gluzman were heard, via a letter they sent from Israel, where they'd returned after the trial.

"For twenty-five years she gradually demolished him emotionally," Yakov Gluzman's parents wrote, "and in the twenty-sixth year she dismembered him physically. By her evil act Rita has ruined the life of her son, whom she left fatherless, and marked him with the stigma of a mother convicted of murder. After we raised Yakov to be a good man and a world-renowned scientist who devoted his life to research and to the benefit of humanity, she suddenly took him away from us."

Parker admonished Rita Gluzman sternly, yet almost understandingly, at her sentencing. Applauding her earlier courage in getting Yakov from behind the Iron Curtain, and complimenting her on her intelligence and success through the years, the judge nonetheless used his sentencing time to wonder out loud just why she'd gone so wrong, what abrupt changes in the once-promising, hard-working Ukrainian had caused her to do something so desperately evil.

"None of us can ever know what transpired between you and your husband. The only thing we know is that nothing that occurred can possibly justify what you did to him. You are a woman of considerable courage, capacity, and accomplishment. For whatever reason, you allowed yourself to disintegrate around the relationship and the pain that grew out of it."

Then, using the federal guidelines before him which outlined mandatory sentences, Parker told Rita of her fate: life, without parole, on the death resulting from domestic violence conviction. Sixty months concurrently on the other three counts. The minor sentences were merely technical; Rita would be remanded immediately to the Federal Correctional Institute in Danbury, Connecticut, to serve the remainder of her days for killing her husband, barring a successful appeal.

Rita had remained quiet throughout the impact statements and Parker's comments, until the close of the hearing. In a trembling voice, she told Parker, "Your Honor . . . I did not do this." Quivering, she continued, "I say this in front of the world."

Rita Gluzman had become the first woman convicted under the Violence Against Women Act for killing her husband. In fact, she was the first person convicted of killing a spouse under the new law. If there was any consolation to her, Rita would at least be in the medium-security Danbury prison, and not on a state prison's death row.

In a demonstration of their support for her, Rita's sister Marianne Rabinowitz joined hands with Ilan and Paula Shapiro as they left the courtroom. "The family is behind her," Rabinowitz told reporters. "She did and built many things in her life that should not be forgotten."

Hochheiser told the reporters that Rita would indeed appeal her conviction and sentence, beginning with the constitutionality of the Violence Against Women Act. As with many federal statutes, it depends on the Interstate Commerce Clause for justification of U.S. intervention. Said Hochheiser, "Crossing state lines to commit a crime has nothing to do with commerce." He and Rosen joined appellate attorney Judd Burstein, another Manhattan lawyer with prime credentials, as they denounced the government's case.

Lou Valvo had one simple comment for the reporters outside on Quarropas Street. "She may have gotten away with murder," the DA said, "if we hadn't worked with the U.S. Attorney's office."

In New City, Mike Bongiorno smiled. It had all worked out well. The DA had sacrificed the publicity that would have come from prosecuting the case of a lifetime because he felt justice would be better served with Rita Gluzman's conviction, even elsewhere, than with a show trial where she could have possibly walked away.

The New York *Daily News'* headline writers couldn't resist, though. "Killer Wife Gets Life," the tabloid told its readers the next day. "Hubby-hack role gets no parole." The sentencing hearing was news throughout New York and overseas.

Two weeks later, Vladimir Zelenin learned of his fate as Judge Parker sentenced the prosecution's star witness for the murder to which he'd confessed. Apologizing again to Yakov Gluzman's family, Zelenin listened as Ilan Gluzman broke his silence to read his victim's impact statement to Parker and the courtroom gallery, which was considerably less crowded than during Rita's hearings.

"The one person [Zelenin] should ask for forgiveness is unable to grant forgiveness because he's lying dead," Ilan began, his hands trembling, his voice strong but cracking. "This murder could not have occurred without Vladimir Zelenin's hands . . . If not for this man, my father would be alive."

The federal sentencing guidelines called for a minimum of twenty-four and a half years for participating with Rita. Parker first took into account Zelenin's cooperation with the prosecutors, then issued his sentence:

twenty-two and a half years in federal prison, to be served concurrently with the state sentence Zelenin would receive in Rockland County Court. He credited Zelenin with the thirteen months he had already spent in jail.

"I cannot draw any meaningful and moral distinction between the conduct of Mrs. Gluzman and your own," the jurist told Zelenin. "I am unable to fathom why you did what you did. You took a life under callous and brutal circumstances."

The judge made one concession to the immigrant. He would be remanded to a federal penitentiary within two hours or so of northern New Jersey, where his sons could visit him. The two boys sat quietly with their grandparents as they watched their father taken away, back to the Rockland jail for another week until his transfer to another prison. The youngest victims of the murder of Yakov Gluzman struck observers as frail, respectful of the court, and devastated by the loss of their father.

For Parker, it was finally over, and his courtroom could return to the less violent cases on the calendar. It was evident the judge was disgusted with both Rita and Zelenin, but he had kept his professional calm. He told his court officer to adjourn until the afternoon, when a drug case was due for pre-trial motions.

In Rockland County Court, for his state sentencing, Vladimir Zelenin was reminded that, although he'd pleaded guilty to murder the year before, and in fact had been sentenced a week before in federal court, he could still change his plea and request a trial. Zelenin passed on the somewhat generous opportunity the American judicial system presented to him, retained his plea, bade farewell to Valvo, and received a twenty-one and a half year sentence, to be served with the federal term.

Epilogue

The great Jimmy Breslin once recounted an anecdote from his days as a young journalist covering a sensational murder trial in middle New Jersey in the 1960s. F. Lee Bailey, fresh off the heels of his victory in winning an appeal for Sam Shepherd, the Cleveland doctor who had been convicted of murdering his wife, was hired by another professional with means who had been charged with killing his wife, to defend him. Bailey argued every point of law successfully, demonized witnesses, and got the man acquitted. After the verdict, Bailey's client turned to the legendary defender and said something to the effect of, "Thank you, Mr. Bailey. I'm grateful you won an acquittal. But I want to tell you, really, I didn't kill my wife."

Bailey turned to his client, according to Breslin's story, with a serious, stern look on his face and provided the man with some hard-earned wisdom. "You didn't do a lot to keep her alive, either."

So it was with Rita Gluzman and the death of her husband.

The case of U.S. vs. Gluzman was an unusual prosecution, as readers of this book know by now. With only the statement of her desperate cousin to prove that she was directly involved in the murder of her husband, Rita was convicted of a novel charge—"crossing state lines to abuse a spouse resulting in death"—that was introduced into criminal law after passage of the 1994 Federal Crime Bill, a piece of legislation enacted to provide more police on the streets of the U.S.

Among the issues debated during the time the Crime Bill was presented in 1994 was whether the federal government would provide a budget for parks and recreation departments across the U.S. to keep basketball courts open late at night for inner-city teenagers. This became known as the fight for "Midnight Basketball," and liberals throughout the U.S. quivered at the thought of this privilege being denied youngsters who might otherwise spend the late hours of their evenings committing petty crimes.

A "throwaway" statute attached to the Crime Bill was the Violence Against Women Act, essentially a sop by its Democratic sponsors to female constituents, particularly in the South, to show concern for the rise of reported incidents of domestic abuse committed by husbands and boyfriends against their wives and girlfriends.

It was ironic then, that Rita Gluzman, a woman, should become the first person charged with and convicted of crossing state lines to abuse and kill a spouse. The legislators who wrote and signed this into law probably envisioned angry men driving in the middle of the night on interstate highways to terrorize female friends, possibly beating them up or, worse, killing them over some small matter.

The prosecutors in the Gluzman case were hardworking, astute, brilliant, career civil servant attorneys whose attention to detail and nonpareil spirit of teamwork resulted in Rita's conviction. The two no-nonsense women in the U.S. Attorney's Office in White Plains who directed the case—Deirdre Daly and Cathy Seibel—spent at least as much time reviewing casework, decisions, and current laws as the highest-priced lawyers in Manhattan and their associates ordinarily would as they brought Rita Gluzman to justice, this in spite of a heavy workload involving drug traffickers, white collar criminals, and others subject to pursuit by the federal law enforcement authorities in the counties north of New York City. Their associate Marjorie Miller suggested to Seibel that Rita might be eligible for prosecution under the Violence to Women Act early on in the investigation, since there is no federal statute for murder. Murder is a state charge, and federal crimes involving death are classified otherwise.

The detectives involved in the Gluzman murder case were also thorough professionals and none had anything in his career or personal history to impede the progress of the investigation, nothing the defense might use to impeach any of their investigation or tesimony. The investigators in the Gluzman murder case weren't covetous of others' jurisdictional catch either: the level of cooperation between Bergen County, Rockland County, and Nassau County was stupendous, though any of the three counties could have charged Rita Gluzman.

The decision to ask for federal help will go down in the annals of law as an act of sacrifice on the part of district attorney Michael Bongiorno. If the U.S. Attorney had lost the case against Rita Gluzman it would have been as damaging as if Rockland had lost in state court over the accomplice rule. But the DA didn't think twice

in transferring the investigation to the U.S. Attorney's
Office once he realized his pursuit of Gluzman on the
state level would result in an expensive trial with no
assurance of a guilty verdict.

From the beginning, almost from the time Sgt. Tom
Goldrick finished his first questioning of Vladimir Zelenin, Rita was the prime suspect in Yakov's killing. Who
else would have wanted Yakov dead? The strength of
Zelenin's statement was damning, even as the detectives
sought to debunk it. Rita was missing, and her disappearance might have lent credibility to her claim to be frightened to death somebody was going to kill her, too—if
it were known Yakov had been killed and butchered.
But it would have been impossible for the widow to
have known about the crime unless she had either been
present, or had commissioned the killing, or if somebody, finally, had called her early Easter Sunday to
inform her of Yakov's murder. Even then, she was locked
in a bitter divorce action with Yakov, and the two hadn't
lived together for more than a year. Why would she
have cared one way or another if Yakov had been murdered? She was safe and sound in her home, and could
have called the police to help her if she had been frightened for her life. After all, Rita had lived in the United
States for nineteen years and knew that New Jersey was
not the Ukraine, or Moscow, so the local police could
be trusted to protect her, or at least not let her end up
dead while in their custody. So her alibi for fleeing was
filled with holes, leading the detectives and the district
attorney to believe her cousin Zelenin's story and suspect her strongly the first week.

The Rockland detectives needed to eliminate possible
other suspects—and find Rita—before they could proceed. Rita's discovery at Cold Spring Harbor had helped
their investigation greatly, once they knew Rita Gluzman

was alive, and hadn't also been a victim of Zelenin's handiwork or a contract killing. Rita's story about her five-day disappearance had convinced Lou Valvo and Steve Colantonio Rita had something to fear other than being killed by the Russian mafia—the motive-less "real killers" a suspect had suggested to police were really the guilty parties to a crime in which he or she was the obvious perpetrator—and the investigators were now free to examine the case with all its variables present.

Others were thought capable of killing Yakov. Had Rita's alibi been more organized, and her discovery less sensational, she might have even convinced the DA, or a judge, or eventually a jury, that she had fled for a good reason. But her story just didn't hold up. So the detectives ruled out the others they thought might have been a party to the killing—Ilan Gluzman, for example. Because he had had a tepid relationship with his father over the last two years of Yakov's life, Ilan was considered by one of the detectives to have had the motive and opportunity to kill Yakov. Perhaps he had acted in concert with his mother, or with Zelenin. After all, Ilan stood to benefit from his father's death as the beneficiary of both his insurance policies and his stock in ECI.

Several interviews with the Gluzman son, however, convinced the detectives that Ilan, first, was truly shaken up over his father's bizarre killing, and second, that his alibi was tight, an accidental late-night sleepover on the New Jersey Turnpike after an evening out with his girlfriend on Staten Island.

There were few other suspects the detectives could examine as they tried to determine the level of Rita's involvement. And as the days passed, Vladimir Zelenin's statements were being corroborated by their interviews with supporting witnesses, like Lenny Huffmann at the CVS drugstore or Yakov's next-door neighbors, who had

seen two people run out early Sunday morning to fix
the car alarm, and the accumulation of evidence such
as telephone records or the Henckel knives.

In its 1996 annual reports, the scientists who run
Cold Spring Harbor Laboratories devoted two pages to
a tribute to the life of Yakov Gluzman. Dr. Winship Herr
wrote, in a letter to trustees and benefactors, that his
friend Gluzman "was a true virologist, who appreciated
that—if one listened carefully—viruses had much to
tell about themselves. He was highly regarded for his
ability to examine experimental problems with clarity
and from unique perspectives; often, he inspired his
colleagues to re-evaluate their scientific assumptions
and interpretations. As a colleague, Yasha had a special
sense of humor. Friends remember him for his famous
bear hugs, which once accidentally broke the ribs of a
colleague . . . His life was too short. We will sorely miss
him, not only for his friendship but also for the discoveries he never had a chance to make."

Lou Valvo sits in his spartan but cozy office on the
third floor of the Rockland County Building in New
City, speaking on the phone to a lawyer for a man just
out on bail from the jail next door. Valvo is smiling
cagily as he explains to the defense attorney why his
client, charged with burglary, is in trouble. "We've got
your client's prints all over the place. Of course he
was there, and we all know he's guilty of something,
counselor!" Valvo laughs; it's almost too easy.

When the lawyer suggests the evidence held by the
DA may not be sufficient to convict his client, Valvo
can't help breaking into his trademark grin and chuck-

les. Valvo's confidence is supreme, and convincing the burglary suspect to plead will save Rockland County the expense of a trial. The conviction of Rita Gluzman has reinvigorated many prosecutors in counties in and around New York City.

Ilan Gluzman continues to run ECI Technologies in East Rutherford, where at this writing he is trying to put the devastating events of the past two years behind him as he resumes a normal life.

Michael Bongiorno was satisfied with the verdicts and the work of his staff. His years in Manhattan had taught him there would be other cases, but the DA was more concerned with justice for Yakov Gluzman than fame in the Rockland courthouse.

Deirdre Daly finished her term as deputy U.S. Attorney for the White Plains office and, after twelve years in public service, entered private practice near her Connecticut home in order to be closer to her family. The prosecutor had little left to prove, and wasn't pursuing book or movie deals.

Cathy Seibel was named Chief U.S. Attorney for the White Plains office in mid-1997, following Daly's departure for private practice.

Steven Colantonio continues to make life difficult for criminals in Rockland County. He teaches karate to students at the junior high school his children attend and runs drug-awareness programs in Rockland County.

Tom Goldrick has participated in several high-level murder and extortion investigations in Bergen County.

Richard Freeman finally made it to Easter dinner with his brother's family. They had stayed up until after midnight, waiting with leftovers, to hear his tale. Modest about his collar, Freeman, who was promoted to sergeant in East Rutherford, says that if his patrol had been fifteen minutes in either direction that day, Zelenin undoubtedly would have completed his dumping and the evidence would have been lost to the Passaic's carp and catfish.

Hilda Kogut was named Woman of the Year by the Rockland Chamber of Commerce. The FBI veteran nears twenty years on the job, and continues to thwart drug smugglers near the Newburgh airport.

Jake Szpicek recruited the nation's first Hasidic Street cop for the Rockland Sheriff's Department. He continues to investigate serious crimes in Rockland County while awaiting the next case where Israel figures in the county's law.

Lawrence Hochheiser continues to defend the unforgiven, and retains his sense of humor.

* * *

Mike Rosen maintains, months after the verdict and sentencing, that the government has yet to prove Rita Gluzman was in Yakov's apartment the night of the murder. Along with Hochheiser, he remains in Rita's corner long after her last bill has been paid.

Rita Gluzman remains incarcerated at the Federal Correctional Institute at Danbury, Connecticut, while her appeal is heard in the U.S. Second Circuit. Her appellate lawyer, Judd Burstein, is challenging the Violence Against Women provision of the Crime Bill in an important commerce clause action.

Acknowledgments

Paul Dinas, Kensington/Pinnacle's editor-in-chief, understood and appreciated the importance of the Gluzman case early on, and deserves highest praise for acquiring and bringing this book to publication. Consulting editor Karen Haas is an outstanding professional whose fine touches made "Severed Relations" much better a book than it would have been without her.

Members of the law enforcement team were generous with their time and helpful in reviewing details with me. Lou Valvo and Mike Bongiorno, Deirdre Daly, Cathy Seibel, Jake Szpicek, and Steve Colantonio each provided the author with insights invaluable to this book, and none put him or herself forth as more essential to the case than any other colleague.

Lawrence Hochheiser and Mike Rosen are tremendous advocates for their clients' rights, and each was generous to me in sharing his insights about the formidable task they faced.

Richard Freeman of the East Rutherford PD, Senior Investigator Tom Goldrick of the Bergen County DA's office, Dr. Mary Anne Clayton, Bergen County Deputy Medical Examiner, and her assistant Coleen McVeigh were of tremendous help. Citizens in Bergen County can sleep comfortably at night with Freeman, Goldrick, Clayton, and McVeigh on the job. Officer Jeff Yannacone of the ERPD was also very helpful to the author.

Tim Costello, friend and photographer, shot most of the post-crime photos for this book, and is a fun professional in every sense of the word. His ample curiosity about the case combined with attention to both the "forest" and the "trees" of the story resulted in the photo spread.

The reporting of Steve Lieberman of the *Reporter-Dispatch* and *Rockland Journal News* was splendid throughout the trial of Rita Gluzman and invaluable to my research. Thanks also to the staff of the *Bergen Record*, Mike Kelly in particular; and to Terri Auchard of the *Record*'s photo department.

Finally, my wife Carisa put up with all that authors go through in completing a book. Our son, Christopher, was splendid: not once did he erase Dad's computer, and at two and a half he's already learned to hit the "save" key.

Tim Hays
New York, NY
November 1997

From the Files of
True Detective
Magazine

HORRIFYING TRUE CRIME
FROM PINNACLE BOOKS